GOD'S PROVISION
in TOUGH TIMES

25 True Stories of God's Provision
During Unemployment and Financial Despair

By

Cynthia Howerter

and

La-Tan Roland Murphy

GOD'S PROVISION IN TOUGH TIMES
Published by Lighthouse Publishing of the Carolinas
2333 Barton Oaks Dr., Raleigh, NC, 27614

ISBN 9781938499449
Copyright © 2013 by Cynthia Howerter and La-Tan Roland Murphy
Cover design by Ken Raney: www.kenraney.com
Book design by Reality Info Systems www.realityinfo.com

Available in print from your local bookstore, online, or from the
publisher at: www.lighthousepublishingofthecarolinas.com

For more information on this book and the authors visit:
http://cynthiahowerter.com
http://latanmurphy.com

Library of Congress Cataloging-in-Publication Data
GOD'S PROVISION IN TOUGH TIMES/ Cynthia Howerter and
La-Tan Roland Murphy 1st ed.

Printed in the United States of America

Praise for *God's Provision in Tough Times*

Everyone has a story. A story is universal. If you live in the United States, Africa, or anywhere else in the world, when faced with a personal tragedy or challenge, human hearts break the same. God can make all the difference in how we overcome such trials, and He can heal our hearts and hurts. Read these amazing stories of how life brought on some tough trials but faith in God gave way to victory. *God's Provision in Tough Times* will certainly give you the courage and confidence that God will help you too!

~ Laine Lawson Craft

Founder of WHOAwomen,
Publisher of *WHOA Magazine for Women,* and
national television talk-show host of the WHOA Show
http://www.whoawomen.com

There is a time for everything,
And a season for every activity under heaven:
A time to be born and a time to die,
A time to plant and a time to uproot,
A time to kill and a time to heal,
A time to tear down and a time to build,
A time to weep and a time to laugh,
A time to mourn and a time to dance,
A time to scatter stones and a time to gather them,
A time to embrace and a time to refrain,
A time to search and a time to give up,
A time to keep and a time to throw away,
A time to tear and a time to mend,
A time to be silent and a time to speak,
A time to love and a time to hate,
A time for war and a time for peace.
What does the worker gain from his toil?
I have seen the burden God has laid on men.
He has made everything beautiful in its time.
He has also set eternity in the hearts of men;
yet they cannot fathom what God has done
from beginning to end.

—Ecclesiastes 3:1-11 (NIV 1984)

TABLE OF CONTENTS

Foreword ix
1. It Comes In Pretty Handy Down Here 1
   James L. Rubart
2. Seeing Past the Mud 9
   La-Tan Roland Murphy
3. An Attitude of Gratitude 19
   Cynthia Howerter
4. Plans.. 27
   Dee Dee Parker
5. Broken.. 37
   Eva Marie Everson
6. Singing in the Pain 47
   La-Tan Roland Murphy
7. Believing God.. 55
   Alycia W. Morales
8. You Can't Outgive God.. 65
   Cynthia Howerter
9. God of All the Years 75
   Cecil Stokes
10. He Makes All Things New 83
    La-Tan Roland Murphy
11. Trusting God, Not the American Dream........................ 91
    Beth K. Fortune
12. Unraveling Relationships 99
    Deborah Raney
13. Facing Forward.. 107
    Cynthia Howerter

14. When Health Issues Affect Employment Options 117
    Carrie Fancett Pagels
15. Trusting for the Future 125
    Ramona Richards
16. The Alpha and Omega Provides 135
    La-Tan Roland Murphy
17. Losing a Job is Personal 145
    Tamara D. Fickas
18. Where Does My Security Lie ... Really? 153
    Dan Walsh
19. Envision Your Blessing 161
    Cynthia Howerter
20. Humility 171
    Felicia Bowen Bridges
21. Recovering from a Lost Call 181
    Roger E. Bruner
22. Where Are We Going? 191
    La-Tan Roland Murphy
23. She Cries on Saturdays 201
    Eddie Jones
24. Life on the Laugh Frontier 211
    Torry Martin
25. Restoration 219
    Cynthia Howerter
26. Meet Our Contributing Writers 229
27. Meet the Authors Cynthia and La-Tan 239

FOREWORD

God sometimes asks us to do things we never imagined.

He surprised me when He told me to write a book about unemployment and financial despair—topics that comprise some of the worst experiences of my life—as a way to encourage others and to offer hope in God's provisional power.

The book began to take shape when I met Eddie Jones of Lighthouse Publishing of the Carolinas. After sharing my family's unemployment story, he encouraged me to write an anthology using not only my experiences, but those of other people as well. A fellow writer told me God gave her the book's name and topic—*God's Provision*—as she listened to the conversation.

The Lord whispered La-Tan Roland Murphy's name when I asked Him to provide a co-author. I didn't know La-Tan well, but as we shared our stories and worked together on the book, we understood why the Lord gave us a writing partnership: we are kindred spirits.

God brought my family through many painful experiences during my husband's unemployment. I am blessed to have witnessed the power of God during such difficult, life-changing times. I am thankful for a godly husband and family members who are willing to share the broken and private experiences of life in order to bless others. Without their prayerful support, this book would not have come to fruition. You will be blessed with contributing writers who candidly share their heartfelt stories of despair and triumph. I hope each story will touch your heart and change your life as you identify with our pain and experience the unique ways in which God provided for each of us during our times of despair.

To God be the Glory!
Cynthia

Why do we struggle to find joy in the midst of financial hardships?

Why do we fall into despair while trying to control our financial future? How do we equip future generations to stand on the promises of God? The answer lies in the failure to recognize our human frailty in light of God's greatness. He is our provider—almighty God—the faithful one. He is the same yesterday, today, and forever. He promises to take care of those who put their faith in Him.

My parents and grandparents never hid their stories of financial hardship. They stood strong on the promises of God and courageously walked through each trial. Because of this, I found courage to share my own struggles. Our children must hear our stories in order to find hope for the future. May they always rest on the promises given in the pages of the Bible, even when their financial circumstances look a mess.

I am thankful to be a part of this powerful book. Each writer has an incredible story that reflects the power of God in the midst of terrible financial hardships. Many people feel as though God has forsaken them. My prayer is for you to find hope within these pages. May you be challenged to trust God and find rest in knowing the One who created you has a good plan beyond your struggles.

All for Him,
La-Tan

1

IT COMES IN PRETTY HANDY DOWN HERE

James L. Rubart

Do not store up for yourselves treasures on earth,
where moth and rust destroy, and
where thieves break in and steal.
But store up for yourselves treasures in heaven,
where moth and rust do not destroy,
and where thieves do not break in and steal.
For where your treasure is, there your heart will be also.

—Matthew 6:19-21 (NIV 1984)

In the movie *It's A Wonderful Life*, George Bailey is talking to his guardian angel, Clarence, about his destitute situation on Christmas Eve, and the subject of money comes up.

"What happened to your wings?" George said.

"I haven't won my wings yet. That's why I'm an angel, second class," Clarence answered.

"I don't know whether I like it very much being seen around with an angel without any wings."

"Oh, I … I've got to earn them, and you'll help me, won't you?"

"Sure, sure. How?"

"By letting me help you," Clarence said.

"Only one way you can help me. You don't happen to have eight thousand bucks on you?"

"Oh, no, no. We don't use money in heaven."

"Oh, that's right. I keep forgetting." George scowled. "Comes in pretty handy down here, Bub!"

***

Do you ever feel like George Bailey? I do. When I watch the movie, I can relate. I feel George's pain.

Didn't used to be that way. When Darci and I got married in May of 1986, we rented a one-bedroom apartment with a swirled pea-green carpet right in back of Edmonds High School for $310 a month. Friday nights in the fall were filled with cheers from the football games, and we figured we could live there for the rest of our lives.

I was on the air at a radio station five minutes from the apartment, and Darci worked as a substitute school teacher. Our combined income was pretty dismal, but it didn't matter. We didn't have any major expenses, and we were young and dumb and madly in love. Money? Didn't need much of it, as neither of us had expensive tastes. So, we didn't think about it much.

A few months later, I started selling air time for the radio station and my income grew. I was on straight commission, so the more I sold, the more I made. After six months, we realized we were living far below our means. So, we moved up and got a two-bedroom apartment that had been built within the last century and had carpet that was a nice tan color.

I continued to sell radio ads, and Darci got a full-time position as a sixth-grade teacher in the Edmonds school district. My career took another leap forward when I accepted a job at a downtown Seattle radio station, and a year after that my dad said I needed the tax break that came with buying a house.

We moved into a beautiful four-bedroom home that cost us $95,000. Not long after, I took a job with another station and my income grew again. Our expenses continued to be far below our income, and after three years, we moved into a bigger home on an acre of land filled with trees. It's the house we still live in today, twenty-two years later.

There were ups and downs as I started my own company in January of '94—and that's part of the deal when you own your own company—but the ups were more frequent than the downs. And, as before, money—or lack thereof—wasn't ever a serious concern.

For eighteen years, we never worried about money, because we continued to live below our means. We didn't have a budget. There was always extra money at the end of the month. We gave money away to friends who needed it. We gave to a variety of charities. We went on nice vacations. Christmas was a bonanza for our two young boys. We stashed money away for retirement.

We went out to dinners and movies and didn't worry about what it cost.

We never, ever, EVER paid a cent of interest on our credit cards.

Ah, yes, those were the days.

Then life changed. I started writing novels. I knew it was the world I needed to step into. A world of highs and lows and glories and deep pain—and an income of eighty cents in my pocket for every book sold. My income dropped and suddenly, money became a major concern.

Would I trade the change I made? Never. When I get an e-mail from a reader telling me one of my novels has changed their life, it's all worth it. All. But these days, we're paying interest on our credit cards. We've had to take out loans to pay for college for our oldest son, and we wonder what's going to happen when our younger son graduates from high school in a year and a half and how in the world we're going to afford it. We wonder how we're going to pay off the home equity loan we took out. We look at our twenty-five-year-old roof and wonder if it can make it through another winter.

Eight thousand dollars would have come in pretty handy for our buddy George Bailey. Eight thousand would come in pretty handy for Darci and me these days…make that eighty.

This is the part of my article where I'm supposed to talk about how we walked into the forest near our home one day last week and found a tree with money growing on it and it solved all our financial woes. Sorry. It was either cut down, or someone got to it first and stripped off all the Benjamins.

You're going to have to get the Cash-Is-Abundant-Again story from the others. But that's okay. Because, I'm guessing some of you are saying, "Nice to know someone else is still going through it. Still wondering where the money is going to come from and if this Mt. Everest of debt can ever be climbed and conquered."

It can. I know it. I believe it. For four reasons:

1. First, God says He will provide. He says He cares more about me than the sparrows, yet He takes care of them. Will I believe that? Yes, I will.

2. Second, my view of money is skewed. I know it. You probably do too, if you logically think about it for a moment. Our vision is myopic, because we live here in the good ol' USA. Do I think often enough of the people who would consider my modest home a mansion? People who would walk in the front door of my house and gasp in wonder at the size and splendor of it? Would they laugh if I told them I *had* to have a cell phone, *had* to have cable TV, and *had* to have a car for both my wife and me? Is having a latte a week too much to ask?

3. Third, I think Jesus is right when He says today has enough worries to keep us occupied—that we don't have to spend our time and energy thinking about tomorrow. So, maybe I'll put off worrying about tomorrow 'til it gets here.

4. Fourth, we don't look at money like God does. I think Clarence is right. They don't use money in heaven. We're

not taking any of it with us. Really. So why are we so
obsessed with it down here? Of course, in complete
transparency, I should tell you of the story of one man
who did take some of it with him:

There was once a man who was Warren Buffet—Bill Gates
wealthy. He'd achieved massive financial success—partly because
he gave much of his money away, and the Lord kept blessing him
with more wealth. Toward the end of his life, he was diagnosed
with cancer and given three months to live.

He prayed to God and said, "Lord, I have served You with my
whole heart all my life, and I am proud of what I've accomplished
with my businesses while on earth. You are my true treasure, yet
I greatly desire to bring some of what I've acquired on earth to
heaven."

The Lord answered and said, "You have been My faithful
servant and a true friend. So, I will make an exception and let
you bring to heaven whatever you can fit into a suitcase."

The man pulled up the Internet, found a huge suitcase online,
and ordered it. While he waited for it to arrive, he converted a
great portion of his wealth into gold bricks. When the suitcase
arrived, he stuffed it full of the gold. Not long after, he passed
away.

Peter the Rock was at the pearly gates when the man
approached, yanking the suitcase along the ground in short
spurts, it was so heavy. When he got to the gate, Peter stared at
him in wonder.

"This is astonishing. Never in the entire history of heaven has God let anyone bring something with them from earth. You and He must have a very special relationship."

"Yes," the man smiled. "We do."

"I don't want to intrude, but might I see what is inside the suitcase?"

"Of course!"

The man was proud of what he'd accomplished on earth and was excited to show Peter the contents. He unzipped the suitcase, threw it open, and stood beaming next to the sparkling bars of gold.

Peter frowned, a puzzled look on his face.

"What's wrong?" the man said.

"I'm just curious," Peter said. "Do you mind explaining why you would bring pavement to heaven?"

Friends, in one sense money matters: we need it for this life. But, in the eternal sense, it is a minor blip on the screen of our lives. And, it is not worth our obsession or constant worry.

If you haven't seen *It's A Wonderful Life,* go rent it. If you have seen the movie, you know George realizes he is the richest man in town—because he has friends who love him. A wife who loves him. Children who love him. I'm hoping you have those things.

I do and am so grateful. I'd add to that a God who calls me His greatest treasure. That alone makes me unfathomably rich.

And you as well.

TIME TO REFLECT ON GOD'S PROVISION

I asked my husband, "Are we going to be okay?"
He said, "Of course we are!"
He told me later how God used that question to establish his
faith that ***yes***, God would provide.

Lord, we thank You that in our weakness, You are strong!

2

SEEING PAST THE MUD

La-Tan Roland Murphy

*But if from there you seek the Lord your God, you will find Him, if
you look for Him with all your heart and with all your soul.
When you are in distress and all these things have happened
to you, then in later days you will return to
the Lord your God and obey Him.
For the Lord your God is a merciful God.
He will not abandon or destroy you or forget the covenant with your
forefathers, which he confirmed to them by oath.*

—Deuteronomy 4:29-31 (NIV 1984)

Drizzly rain gently landed on the windshield, making its watery
way downward. Beloved gospel music blared on the radio. My
parents loved music; they also enjoyed taking road trips together.
This trip was a special one, because they would be visiting my
brother and sister-in-law, and that filled their hearts with sheer
joy. Though disappointed because of the rain, they determined
not to allow a little bit of drizzle to interfere with their long-
awaited trip. The music lifted their spirits above the gloominess

of the weather. Nothing could put a damper on the excitement in their hearts.

As they passed under a bridge, everything suddenly went dark. Without any warning, the windshield was covered with thick, murky mud. With his vision impaired, my father struggled to keep control of the car. No longer able to see the road ahead, sheer panic set in. My father was only able to see through the side windows and the rearview mirrors, as he and Mother continued blindly through traffic. While whispering hope-filled prayers that God would help them get to safety, fear gripped their humanity with a vice. Little did they know, the drizzle would be their blessing in disguise, as it cleared a few spots on the windshield, enabling them to maneuver through six lanes of traffic, off the interstate, and onto the roadside. With hearts pounding, they sat frozen in place. They were stunned by the fact that they had made it to safety, given their perilous circumstances. Disbelief consumed them as they realized that someone had dumped a bucket of mud from the bridge as they passed under.

Perhaps they felt the same way on the day they heard the dreadful news that they had lost everything they had worked for their entire lives. Their view of a blessed future muddied over with the dreadful news of impending foreclosure. My father was devastated. My mother stood in the kitchen, the foreclosure notice in hand, as one pleading prayer after another slammed into her questioning heart: *How could this be happening? How can we possibly lose it all at retirement age? Lord, we have worked so hard through the years. We have been faithful givers. Lord ... not our home. But Lord, we love this home. We helped the builder draw up the plans in order to truly make it our own. But, this is our dream home; please Lord, don't ask us to give it up. We tended this land together and raised our family here. How can this be happening?*

Then, with much determination, they forced their fleshly humanity to turn to something more secure—something they had leaned hard into for years; something they would need to cling to now, more than ever before—their faith in the God who provides.

My father, now sixty-two years old, was devastated. My mother, a strong woman of faith, dug deep within the pockets of her hurting heart to find a remnant of encouragement that would lift his head upward, refocusing him beyond the muddy mess to the blessings in their lives. Time and time again, my mother pointed my father's down-cast spirit upward. While my father's vision was blurred by the mud on the windshield of his mind, Mother's courageous spirit fought to keep him focused on the new path ahead of them.

A realist, Mother knew full well this journey through financial despair would be filled with insecurities for daily provision. Her faith in God was strong due to her ability to remember the way God had taken care of them in previous tough times. Courage rose up. Her fears cried out as a result of her own deep and personal panic. Each time, she pushed them back down. When fear crept into their minds, threatening to paralyze and muddy their joy and hope in the Lord, they fought those feelings—not in their own human strength, but in the strength of the Lord. In doing this, they steadied their frazzled emotions and leaned hard into the truth of God's word.

Time became a pressing issue when they were told to leave the home and property within two to three weeks. How sad it was to witness their desperate search for a home at such a vulnerable age of life. They went from trailer park to trailer park before finally settling into an old, worn-down house built around the late 1800s. How sad it was to walk through each room of the old house, viewing the ground through the plank flooring, and seeing the claw-foot bathtub that was nearly falling through the foundation. There was no heat or air-conditioning, and with the large rooms and high ceilings, this set the stage for physical discomfort.

The home was owned by a friend of the family. He knew my parents well and respected their reputation in the community. If it had not been for him and his family, my parents could have been homeless. Thanks to this kind gentleman, my parents were able to rent the house at an affordable rate per month. He told them that they were welcome to live there as long as they needed to. He also offered an opportunity to buy the house and one acre of land at a bargain rate, if they could get back on their feet financially.

In much the same way that God had provided a drizzly rain to fall on the windshield of the car, giving my parents a tiny view to get to safety, God provided a home for them. My brother and brother-in-law helped repair the old house to make it livable. Though it was far from being their dream house, my mother said to my father, "It's not the house that makes a home, *we* make the home." And so they did …

The smell of fresh coffee brewing drew us in as we opened the back porch screen door. The sweet smell of baking cakes wafted through the air, causing one to forget about the aesthetic surroundings or the fact that the house had no air-conditioning or proper heating units.

To this day, the one thing that stands out in my mind is the fact that my parents did not allow their circumstances to dictate their lives or their ability to extend hospitality. When visitors came by, they were wrapped in the sweet gift of hospitality that came so naturally to both of my parents. Each guest was greeted with a smile, a hug, and delicious food. My parents never made mention of, or apologized for, their meager home. The love they extended made everyone feel warm inside, even when the temperature of the house said otherwise.

Their neighbors could not believe how lush the garden was. It was by far the best garden my parents ever had. My father was so proud of how large the cabbage was. The carefully planted rows of beans, onions, potatoes and watermelon grew in blessed abundance. Even the fig tree that had appeared completely dead when they moved into the house sprung forth. The tall stalks of corn danced in the warm, southern breeze as though to say, "Our God is worthy to be praised!"

The most difficult things to leave behind at the farm were the beautiful fig trees. They had been a source of giving for my parents. Sugary-sweet fig preserves proudly peeked through mason jars and lined my mother's country cupboard. As silly as it might sound to some, my parents were sad to leave those fig trees behind. I suppose when a person has the heart of a giver pounding inside of them like my parents did—especially after having lost all of their material possessions—it must feel as though they have nothing left to give. Even still, they were always ready and willing to give God glory for the things He had done for them. This gave hope for the future that God would continue to provide.

Had it been a "coincidence" that their new house just happened to have a fig tree behind it? My parents would quickly tell you no. By summer, it boasted huge, juicy figs. Because of this, they felt God had brought them to the old house, and this gave them peace to settle in.

Though times were difficult, through it all, God was there. My parents were very conscious of the fact that He had never taken His holy eyes off of them or their situation. He had lovingly provided for all of their needs, far more than they could have ever imagined. They were quick to acknowledge Him and give praise for all the things He had done for them. Whining just wasn't an option.

My mother always said, "One day my ship will come in." In my heart, I know with deep certainty that her verbal act of faith was the reason why the real estate investor came to their door eleven years later, desiring to purchase the old house and the land it sat on. He offered enough money to buy a comfortable, small, brick home with central heat and air-conditioning on almost an acre of land. And would you say it is a coincidence if I told you there was a fig tree in the back yard? Yes, a beautiful, lush, green fig tree, billowing with plump, delicious figs—proof that God cares about the desires of our heart. The home was warm in the winter and cool in the summer—a detail most of us take for granted. God took care of my parents' every need way before they knew they had one.

Shortly after moving in, my father became bed-bound. His hospital bed sat in the living room, facing the front window of the house. I am sure he reflected back through the years to the goodness of God he spoke so freely about to us children as he looked out through that window at Mother's potted pansies in the winter and petunias in the summer. Even when he faced the uncertainty of not knowing how things would work out, he was quick to say, "I know God will make a way."

The drizzly rain we are so often inclined to complain about may turn out to be a godly provision intended to help us see our way. When the stress in our lives becomes intense and we can't see things clearly, we do not have to go at it alone. God longs to help us. He longs for us to invite Him on our life journey. He has a much better plan in place, just like He had a perfect plan beyond the muddy circumstances in my parents' lives. That plan would ultimately enable my mother to care for my bed-bound father for two and a half years before his grand journey to his heavenly home.

I think most of us would fail to notice the small details of God's provisions we encounter each day, because we tend to look more to the checkbook as our gauge for provisional proof. When we can't see the hand of God at work, we often lose heart, failing to see past the mud on the windshield.

The things my parents went through have given my husband and me strength and hope while facing our own financial difficulties. We have renewed determination to seek God with all of our hearts. We have discovered time and time again that when we seek the Lord with all our heart in every circumstance of life,

He is faithful to provide for us in amazing and unexpected ways. He is the God who does not forget those who put their trust in Him.

Trust Him today. He is providing for you too, my friend. Keep looking past the mud.

Time to Reflect on God's Provision

It's the hard road that bruises my feet the most,
but it's also the hard road that toughens me up the most.
Thank You, Lord, that there is a purpose in this pain.

For I am the Lord your God,
who takes hold of your right hand and says to you,
do not fear; I will help you.

—Isaiah 41:13 (NIV)

3

AN ATTITUDE OF GRATITUDE

Cynthia Howerter

Beware that you do not forget the Lord your God
By not keeping His commandments,
His judgments, and His statutes which I command you today,
Lest when you have eaten and are full,
And have built beautiful houses and dwell in them;
And when your herds and your flocks multiply,
And your silver and gold are multiplied,
And all that you have is multiplied,
When your heart is lifted up, And you forget the Lord your God
Who brought you out of the land of Egypt,
from the house of bondage.

—Deuteronomy 8:11-14 (NKJV)

My husband and I taught our children that everything we have in life is a gift from the Lord, and just like we thank someone when they give us a gift, we need to be thankful and express gratitude to the Lord when He bestows a blessing upon us. When our children failed to thank someone for a gift, we gave them a choice: either thank the person or return the gift. It's a lesson my husband and I neglected to apply during one prosperous year when our successes paved the way for self-reliance and self-credit.

In February 2008, my family and I watched our lives abruptly change from financial uncertainty to having little financial concern when my husband, Tim, accepted a vice-president's position at a company in Cleveland, Ohio.

The current vice-president had been diagnosed with a potentially fatal illness, and the company wanted to train Tim to take over this man's responsibilities. While our family was elated for Tim's new opportunity that advanced him further up the corporate ladder, our joy was tempered with sadness for this man's grave diagnosis.

Before we could place our Pittsburgh house on the market, we needed to complete the renovations that were already in progress. It made the most sense for me to stay behind and oversee the improvements while Tim worked in Cleveland. Tears stung my eyes as I watched Tim pack his suitcases. When he gave me a final hug before getting into his car to move to another state without me, the lump in my throat made it difficult to whisper "good-bye." Several days later Tim called to tell me that he found an apartment near his new office.

Because we had the financial means to pay for rent and make our mortgage payment, Tim and I had no need to ask God for help. However, we failed to recognize that it was God who was the true provider of Tim's job and income. In not acknowledging or thanking God for His generosity, we took the first giant step in leaving our Heavenly Father out of our very blessed lives.

Two months after Tim began working in Ohio, we placed our Pittsburgh house on the market and settled into a routine where Tim lived in Cleveland during the week and drove home every weekend while I stayed in our unsold house. Our weekends were busy as we tried to catch up with the house and yard work—in between realtors showing prospective buyers the house. We stopped attending church, believing the excuse that our weekends were so hectic we didn't have the time to go—not even for an hour. The truth is, we gave our time to the things we felt were important. Unfortunately, God was no longer in that category.

Our two cars had seen their best days and needed to be replaced—something we'd delayed doing with two children attending college. Tim purchased an SUV that could handle the snowy northeast Ohio winter and, because we were celebrating our thirtieth wedding anniversary, he told me to purchase whatever car I wanted within a certain price range. I'd had my eye on a sporty red Nissan Altima. After leaving the dealership, I thanked my hubby by taking him for a quick spin before stopping at our favorite ice cream shop. I should have sunk to my knees thanking God for generously providing us with the ability to buy not one but two new cars, but God wasn't even in my thoughts.

During the summer, both of our children needed to set up apartments before they began graduate studies. Once that was accomplished, the kids and I took a vacation, traveling to historical sites throughout Virginia. Tim and I provided the financial means for these endeavors—or at least, we believed this provision came from us.

I stayed with Tim at the apartment occasionally, but its eleventh-floor location and small size made me feel closed in and trapped. I was equally uncomfortable outside the building because of its urban setting. I longed for the roomy freedom of our Pittsburgh house and neighborhood. However, as disagreeable as it felt to be in the apartment, staying alone in our house with only memories of happy family times for company wasn't much better. My heart ached with loneliness and I cried frequently, but never once did I cry out for God's help or ask for His wisdom.

By now, it was late summer. It had been six months since Tim moved to Cleveland, and I couldn't stand being alone any longer. I packed up our two Himalayans and drove to the Cleveland apartment. Within two days, the cramped urban setting made me feel like a caged animal. Tim urged me to take our cats and return to Pittsburgh. For the first time in months, Tim's salary failed to take care of a need. This should have set off warning bells—but all was silent until the next morning.

Tears ran down my cheeks as I drove out of the apartment complex in my red Nissan and, for the first time in months, I prayed earnestly. "Lord, You gave Tim a job in Cleveland. We need to buy a house there, but we can't until we sell our Pittsburgh house. Not a single person has placed a bid on it after all these months, and I don't understand why. Tim and I want to be together. We hate being apart, but we're in limbo. Please talk to me, God. Please tell me what to do."

God was there—even after months of being ignored. His voice was so soft that I almost didn't realize it was Him.

"Trust," He whispered.

Two weeks later, I ran into a friend of ours from church. As we spoke, an odd look crossed his face. "Cynthia, God just spoke to me and I'm to tell you this: The reason your house isn't selling is because God will be bringing Tim back to Pittsburgh."

I was stunned. I knew the only way Tim would return to Pittsburgh was if he lost his job in Cleveland. That definitely was not what I wanted to hear, so I gave our friend's words no further consideration. I ignored God.

On the first day of December, I inexplicably recalled our friend's comment that God would be bringing Tim back to Pittsburgh. I told myself that it was preposterous that God would give Tim a new job only to take it away. From then on, our friend's words returned to me daily, but I continued to pay no heed to them. Because I didn't like it, I ignored God's message until He laid it right in front of me.

Twelve days later, in the middle of a Friday afternoon, I heard the garage door open. Tim was back in Pittsburgh—jobless. The vice-president whom Tim had been hired to replace experienced a miracle: he recovered from his illness. Tim was let go—the victim of another person's miracle and the deep 2008 recession. Tim and I rejoiced that this man faced a wonderful fresh start, but our hearts were heavy with grief because our promising future was now bleak.

The prosperity that blinded us was gone, and we realized that what we truly needed wasn't money, but God. After asking for forgiveness for turning away from the Lord, we determined to keep a renewed focus on God's provisional power by re-establishing our prayer life. We began worshipping the Lord every Sunday and committed to remain grounded in His word.

We sensed God telling us to keep our house on the market and, three weeks after Tim returned to Pittsburgh, it sold for a good price. Once the buyer learned about Tim's job loss, they offered to let us stay in the house for several months, which gave Tim time to job hunt and allowed us to find other housing. Although Tim did not qualify for any unemployment benefits due to a technicality, he received severance pay that paid all of our bills for a while. It was clear to Tim and me that it was God who was providing for us.

In the midst of the austere winter of unemployment, we began a habit of gratefulness by starting each day thanking God for ten good things in our life before we got out of bed. With two kids in college, a mortgage payment, ongoing expenses, and no income other than the temporary severance pay, our first gratitude prayer was challenging until we realized we needed to be grateful for the small things in life that are easily overlooked.

I prayed while Tim listened. "Father, we thank You that we are both breathing and that our children are alive. We're thankful to be in our own bed. And, Lord, if we're lying here in our own bed, then it means we're still in our house. And if we're in our house, then we're still in our neighborhood. And if we're in our neighborhood, then our church is nearby. We thank You for these blessings. Thank You for loved ones who pray for us. Thank You that our house is heated and our kitchen is stocked with food. Our hearts are filled with gratefulness to You, Father, for providing each of these blessings."

"That's only nine," Tim whispered.

I paused for a moment, listening to chickadees chirping in the shrubs outside our window. Once our abundance was gone and we were left with little, God had our full attention. Now He used small things to teach us gratitude. "Thank you, God, for the chickadees and their song, because they remind us that You are the source of all provision. Lord, please accept our gratefulness and forgive our sins. Be our guide each day of our life. Amen."

"You know, once we get out of bed and go about our day, we're going to discover more of God's blessings." Tim looked into my eyes. "We can never stop looking for them."

Smiling, I nodded. "We can never stop thanking God for them."

Although Tim and I did not know it the morning of our first gratitude prayer, we would face twenty more months of unemployment before Tim found another job. Our new attitude of gratefulness that intentionally looked for God's provision enabled Tim and me to discover the Lord's blessings in all situations. The ability to recognize God's blessings and our sincere gratitude for them kept us from giving up. We knew that God was truly with us.

Time to Reflect on God's Provision

Why is it, Lord, that enough never seems like enough—
especially when my heart is far from You?

Come to the waters;
and you who have no money,
come, buy and eat!
Come, buy wine and milk
without money and without cost.
Come, all you who are thirsty,
why spend money on what is not bread,
and your labor on what does not satisfy?
Listen, listen to me, and eat what is good,
and your soul will delight in the richest of fare.
Give ear and come to me;
hear me, that your soul may live.
I will make an everlasting covenant with you,
my faithful love promised to David.

—Isaiah 55:1-3 (NIV 1984)

4

PLANS
Dee Dee Parker

"For I know the plans I have for you," declares the Lord,
"plans to prosper you and not to harm you,
plans to give you hope and a future."
—Jeremiah 29:11 (NIV)

Fall in the Blue Ridge Mountains had never been more beautiful. I sat on my deck, worshipping the Lord, stirred by His vibrant splashes of color as a cup of hot apple cider drew the chill from my fingers. Pots of purple, yellow, and burgundy mums waltzed up the deck stairs. My eyes traced the rise of smoke from the neighbor's chimney as the sweet scent of apple wood wrapped me in a cocoon of peace. All was well in my little hollow as I rested from a busy day's labor. Hymns proclaiming harvests safely gathered in and families gathering together to ask the Lord's blessing filled my soul and spilled from my lips.

Earlier, I took pies rich with nutmeg and cinnamon, made from the pumpkins that survived my late summer harvest, to the neighborhood food pantry. A wheelbarrow stood against the springhouse, emptied of its fading orange orbs, once proud pumpkins that had been the centerpiece of our fall display. The pumpkins were gifts to the animals that lived in the thickets behind our home. My mind's eye pictured the woodland creatures enjoying their own Thanksgiving feast from my garden bounty.

Having finished my fall chores, my thoughts turned to the coming Christmas season and a planned trip to my attic for holiday decorations. I sipped the last drops of cider, said goodbye to the glorious season of plenty, and dreamed of snowflakes and the perfect tree.

There was only one little snag in my peaceful cocoon. My voice.

***

"Would you please repeat what you said? It sounds like you are whispering." This was not the first time I had heard these words while talking on the phone the past two weeks. My voice was raspy due to what I felt was overuse at work and the strain of extra choir rehearsals scheduled in preparation for our Christmas cantata.

My first course of action was to rest my voice and only use it when absolutely necessary. It helped that the choir director, Jim, was also my husband, and he assured me he was confident I knew the music well enough to miss practice for a few weeks.

With a plan in place, I began to hope everything would be back to normal in no time at all. Well … you know the old adage about best-laid plans. At the end of three weeks, my voice had not improved. The last straw was when the technician from the dental lab said, "Dee Dee, I'm sorry, I can't understand what you are saying."

Thinking my problem could be handled quickly with antibiotics or a throat spray, I made an appointment with my family doctor. However, the appointment only worked to frustrate me more. My doctor told me he wasn't qualified to help with my problem, so I left his office with another appointment—this time with an ear, nose, and throat specialist, or ENT for short—in the next city.

Despite this new hitch in my plans, I still thought my throat problem was minor—the specialist would have my voice back in good shape in a short time. The consultation with the ENT only furthered this conviction. He found what he thought was a polyp, most likely resulting from vocal overuse. I felt confident in his diagnosis. At the specialist's recommendation, I was admitted to the hospital for surgery and a biopsy. The doctor said he would have the results in a few days; nothing to worry about, he assured me.

Jim called the dentist I worked for and explained I was on vocal rest but would be back to work in a few days. I had to be creative in order to communicate with my husband and children, so I resorted to using an Etch-A-Sketch© as my means of communication. I soon found out that in the ways of child-rearing, the grainy, scrawled letters did not wield the same power as a few strong words flowing from Mama's mouth.

The doctor's office called but only to remind me to not use my voice. The impish joy in my children's eyes when they heard the doctor had ordered more vocal rest did not escape me. I started writing in capital letters when I wanted my Etch-A-Sketch© words to be more meaningful.

Finally, after waiting what seemed like a lifetime, the doctor called and asked me to come to his office and to bring my husband with me. A seed of worry planted in my mind. My doctor told me it wasn't a polyp but the first tumor of its kind on a vocal cord. He had scheduled an appointment with a specialist at the teaching hospital at the University of Virginia; I was also told the doctors at UVA were very interested in my tumor due to its rare nature.

Jim again called my employer, and I took sick leave. Tingles of anxiety ran the length of my body as I worried about running out of paid leave and having to dip into savings. I hoped the doctors wouldn't want to order an expensive surgery that would require a long convalescence.

The University of Virginia was six hours from home, which meant I would be away from my children during the days leading up to Christmas and would end up missing the church play practices, holiday parties, and shopping. Yet another seed of worry took root in my mind. Who would make the Santa cookies and address the holiday cards?

Jim and I started out to UVA with a huge basket of cards from our church family, and every time we stopped he read aloud a few cards to boost our morale. As we arrived at the hospital and approached the building, we encountered a man smoking a cigarette through his stoma, an artificial opening to his trachea. A chill shot straight down my spine—would I end up with a hole in my throat? Jim could sense my mounting apprehension and put a reassuring hand on my shoulder.

Of course, the doctors wanted to operate. I was terrified. Even though my fears closed in on me, the surgery went well and I came home to pick up my Etch-A-Sketch© once again. Sitting back on my couch, I wondered if it would feel like I was singing if I drew musical notes next to the words of Christmas carols.

At my follow-up appointment, my surgeon, Dr. Johns, said they needed to operate again—the tumor was back. Discouraged, I called my employer, and he graciously gave me added sick leave. Our savings was getting smaller and smaller, and I was scared our money would run out at the same time as my employer's patience. Missing out on Christmas cheer was the least of my worries now.

Four more surgeries followed in as many months. It was a bleak time, but I steadied myself again and again with my faith and prayed that it would pass. As I was wheeled into the last surgery, Dr. Johns appeared at my bedside in a hospital gown and bed slippers. I said, "Dr. Johns, you forgot to get dressed this morning!" He laughed and said he was a patient in the hospital himself but would be filming my surgery. My laughter at both doctor and patient in hospital gowns helped ease my worry over the surgery outcome.

My husband of forty-four years says I have my degree in talking. Upon being allowed to speak after the final surgery, I cried at hearing my voice. *Hello again, old friend.* The nurses said my long-term prognosis was hopeful. In the meantime, they encouraged me to take sign language. In the end, Dr. Johns had to break the news to me. It wouldn't be possible to return to my old job; he said I would have to find a job that required little talking. Disappointed and unsure, I resigned my receptionist position at the dentist's office.

My convalescence started off well and everything seemed on track for a steady recovery, until I had to have an emergency back operation. It wasn't long after the anesthesia wore off that I realized how limited my options had become. After my vocal cord surgeries, I knew I could find a job that required minimal talking; but now with the added back surgery, I couldn't sit or stand for long periods of time. I was told there was nothing I could do in the job market.

This truly felt like my lowest point. I had survived multiple surgeries only to be told I was unemployable. What would my family do? Without my salary, the growing mounds of medical bills would soon fill my college trunk. My only option was federal benefits. My family prayed for help as I applied for Social Security Disability. I started the long and bureaucratic process, praying it would be resolved quickly. Despite my hopes, I knew that being only twenty-eight years old would not help my cause.

The government denied my first application and I had to start the process over again. We had been without my income for twenty-two months and were falling further behind with bills. The heartache of unemployment welled up inside me. I had been denied benefits and was not released to return to work. What would become of me? To lessen my fears, I repeated scriptures that held promises of a faithful Savior.

Dr. Johns and his colleagues at UVA sent letters to the disability determination board and after several months, I was scheduled for an appointment with a doctor chosen by the Social Security Administration. This doctor was not allowed to discuss his findings with me and said that in a short time I would receive a letter telling me of the board's decision.

Leaving the doctor's office, I felt hope that the situation would soon be settled. Each day of that first week, I hurried to the mailbox, only to find it empty. The waiting created an uneasiness in me I had never felt before, causing waves of nausea to engulf my body. There was no peace of mind or rest for my soul. Constant pacing became commonplace, robbing me of any physical comfort. Two more months passed before the favorable decision came; thank the Lord, I had been approved for disability benefits. Despite the relief I felt when I received the decision, it wasn't the same as going back to work.

Looking at the country's current economic slump and rising unemployment rates, I realize that many others are now feeling the way I did so long ago. I desperately wanted to return to work and it was unbearable when I was unable to do so. My monthly social security payment was far less than my job salary, as I am sure unemployment benefits are for out-of-work Americans.

My family had to learn to adjust to less money, but we found inventive ways to live less expensively. Meal planning became a must and coupons became a way of life. We had yard sales for the children's outgrown clothes and were able to purchase new clothes by watching for sales. Christmas became a blessed time with more emphasis placed on Christ's birth than on the giving of gifts. We found we could live on less and still have a great quality of life. We found that our faith could sustain us when our bank account could not.

During the long months of being out of work, I found a deeper trust in Jehovah-Jireh, my provider. I am living the plan God chose for my life with gratitude and peace. My prayer for those who are, or will, walk this path of unemployment, is that they will know His ever-present care in their time of need.

Time to Reflect on God's Provision

There is no shame we have gone through that God Himself has not gone through for us.

Then you will lift up your face without shame;
you will stand firm and without fear.

—Job 11:15 (NIV)

5

BROKEN
Eva Marie Everson

I was young and now I am old,
yet I have never seen the righteous forsaken
or their children begging bread.

—Psalm 37:25 (NIV)

I remember thinking, six months before the world turned pear-shaped, how awful it would be to lose everything. Of course, I didn't see how it could happen. Not to us. We both had good jobs. We made good salaries. We lived in a spacious brick house, located in a Georgia neighborhood of lush acre lots filled with playing children, frisky dogs, and lazy cats. Every morning school buses rambled down the streets and moms and dads headed for work. On Saturday mornings lawn mowers cut neat lines, mothers carried groceries in from the car. By evening, smoke curled into the air from grills where steaks and burgers cooked. Friends gathered, sat in lawn chairs, sipped on sweet iced tea, laughed, and relaxed. And Sundays were spent in worship.

Life was ideal.

Nothing could break that apart. I knew it. Deep down, I knew it. *But wouldn't it be awful,* I thought, *if it did?*

Spring of 1992 came. I returned home from work one day and told my husband Dennis I didn't feel well. He suggested I lie down. I did, thinking I'd take a half-hour nap, wake up, cook dinner, and be fully well by morning. I was wrong. I wasn't better the next day or the next or the next. Over the following months, my life became defined by doctor's offices, laboratories, and hospitals. As my life went south, my income went with it.

Then, in October, my husband's brother-in-law, John,* called from Florida. Like my husband, he owned a landscape business. The house-building business in Central Florida, he told us, was booming. There was more work than he could shake a stick at. He suggested we come down and see for ourselves.

While my sister-in-law and I drove around looking at apartments and houses for rent, our husbands went over the logistics of combining their businesses. We returned to Georgia and prayed together for God's guidance. We also discussed the opportunity with friends and our pastor, all of us coming to the same conclusion: we were to move to the Orlando area.

By the end of December, we had moved. I continued to battle physical issues, but with my husband's financial windfall, I was free to stay home and concentrate on getting better. Life couldn't have been sweeter.

Until ...

About three months went by when Dennis came home to our apartment, looking fairly glum. "What's wrong," I asked him.

"I caught John stealing today."

"Are you sure?"

"I'm fairly sure."

"But you have to know for certain before you make an accusation like that."

"You're right," he said, brightening. "Maybe I'm wrong."

A few days later, the scene repeated itself. This time, my husband said he'd confronted his brother-in-law. John denied everything, but my husband knew what he'd seen.

Long weeks went by. Tension grew between the business partners and, with that, the family. I couldn't believe the turn of events. We'd come to Florida with such hope. Now, not only was my health increasingly getting worse, but my husband's family had divided and our finances were a wreck.

And then the letter came. The one that included a stipend and a "hope we can still be family, but I'm taking it all back" kind of letter. We'd awoken that morning with my husband owning half a business, and by breakfast, we were both jobless.

That day was also rent day. I sat at the desk, pulled out the checkbook, wrote the check with a shaking hand, and handed it to my husband. "Take it to the complex office," I said. "The walk will do you good."

Dennis looked at me like I had two heads, but he took the check and walked out the door with a sigh. I knew from experience it would take him about ten minutes to walk to the office, about ten back. Within twenty-five, he should be home, where he would sit, stare blindly ahead, and try to figure out what we were going to do for *next* month's rent.

Not to mention next week's meals. For those twenty-five minutes, I sat on the floor, buried my face in my hands, and cried out to God.

Dennis didn't return for an hour. By then, I was frantic, fearing crazy things. But one look at his face when he entered, and I knew something good had happened. "I got a job," he said.

"What? Where?"

"When I walked into the office, Faye said, 'You look like you lost your best friend.' I told her she was close. Then I told her what happened. You know me; I never talk about my personal life like that. But something inside told me to, so I did. She said there's an opening for a landscape supervisor on site. It doesn't pay much. Hardly anything at all, but there's a decrease in our rent, and the hours are from six to two, which means I can try to rebuild my landscape business after two o'clock."

For a minute I felt as if everything would be all right. It didn't take me long to see that *nothing* was all right. My health was crashing; I had consistent chest pains, shortness of breath, dizziness, and tingling up and down my left arm. I felt as if an elephant was sitting on me, crushing the life out of me. Constantly. I didn't want my husband to know, though. He had enough to worry about. Instead, I told the one and only friend I'd made since coming to Central Florida.

Lori.

Lori was from New York. Her heritage—Italian. Italian Catholic, to be exact. Pretty much every caricature of New York Italian Catholics you've ever seen in the movies ... well, that was Lori. For one, Lori didn't mind saying *whatever* was on her mind. For another, when it came to friendship, she was fiercely loyal. When I called her to tell her I thought I was having a heart attack, she ran through my front door before I hung up the phone. She drove through traffic like an Indy 500 racer, pushed her way through the mire of the emergency room, and got me "to the back" in record time. Of course, when they drew blood she passed out, but she'd managed to make me laugh when I could hardly find a reason to smile.

Lori knew one thing about this crazy Southern friend of hers: I was a woman of faith. So, when social services came to my hospital room and told me what we'd need to do—in our financial state—to get on Medicaid, I felt more embarrassed for God than for me. After all, what kind of God would allow His children to leave their beautiful home, their friends, their well-constructed lives for ... this?

The degradation didn't stop there, however. After being released from the hospital, I drove to the address scribbled on a business card. In one of the longest hours of my life, I sat in a room with grease-stained walls, surrounded by folks—many who'd apparently lost their showers and bathtubs—and then later across from a woman who looked at me as if I were the scum of the earth. I returned to our apartment with a stack of paperwork, not only for Medicaid, but for food stamps and welfare as well.

As the weeks dragged on, my husband worked harder than three men. Still, we grew financially further and further behind. I recall the day when I sat in the middle of the living room floor, folding towels. They stood like the Leaning Tower of Pisa, waiting for the final fluff and fold, followed by my taking them to the linen closet. Just then my husband walked in, covered in sweat and grass and holding the mail. One envelope had been ripped open; he held a tri-folded letter in his hand.

"We've qualified," he said. "Food stamps. Medicaid. Welfare."

Torn between horrified and grateful, I balled my hand into a fist and socked the stack of towels, sending them flying across the room. I fumed. I screamed. I beat that same fist into the floor. How could we hold our heads up now? How could God do this to us? His *children*? I found myself crying as the Hebrews cried out to God, "Did you bring us out of Egypt only to have us die in the desert?"

But Lori, who I'd so wanted to *impress* with my strong faith, had a different spin on it. "Isn't it something," she said. "If Dennis hadn't walked the rent check to the office when he did, he wouldn't have a job where he can work part-time *and* build his business. And if you hadn't had the issue with your heart, you wouldn't have been in the hospital, and the social services lady wouldn't have come to see you. You wouldn't have even *thought* to file for financial aid. Looks to me like God is being very good to you."

She was right, of course. I had no more temper tantrums, although I refused to shop with food stamps unless it was after ten o'clock, when there were only a few people in the stores. And I cringed with every medical appointment when I was forced to write *Medicaid* in the square under "insurance."

Still, God worked in me. He broke me down so He could build me back up. He showed me that I might not like *how* I got ad, but I wouldn't *beg* for it, just like He'd promised in His

Word. He also taught me a lot about trusting His ways. Strange as they may be.

It was during this time that I returned to an old love: reading. With the closing of each book, I'd think, *I could have written that.*

Soon, I bought a few composition books and, propped up in bed or in the recliner, I jotted my own stories along the thin blue lines. After a while, as my health returned, I sat at the computer and typed more stories. Better stories.

I had *no* idea God was growing an award-winning, multi-published writer. More than that, He strengthened my marriage, which I'd thought strong enough. He deepened my faith, which I'd thought deep enough. And, He bonded me to a young New York Italian Catholic who would soon move away to South Florida, but who would forever be my dear friend.

As time went on, Dennis's business grew. He left the employment of the apartment complex, we moved to a house (and eventually another and another), and we prospered. While we no longer count every penny (or roll them, for that matter), we remain frugal. We are now more aware of those who are less fortunate than us, and we are open to God's leading when it comes to aiding. To being His feet and hands. His dollars and cents. I never want to forget that.

I look back on those days, nearly twenty years ago, and I wonder sometimes how we managed to live through them. But, we did. One memory that stands out above the others involves the afternoon I went to the drug store to get my prescriptions filled. Two older women stood in front of me in the line. One said to the other, "Am I on Medi*caid* or Medi*care*?"

"Medicare."

"Well, how do you know the difference?" the first woman asked.

"Medi*care* is for old people like us and Medi*caid* is for poor people."

Like me, I thought.

But I wasn't poor. I was *broke, but I wasn't poor.* In spite of the rift in my husband's family, we still had family on both sides who always let us know they were "there for us." I had a husband who loved me, children who grew in their faith, their studies, and their talents, and a budding infatuation with *words.*

Like these.

Like His.

Like *Him.*

*Name has been changed.

TIME TO REFLECT ON GOD'S PROVISION

My friends often asked me, "How can you be so positive during
such stressful circumstances?"
I would tell them: "When you lift your empty self up to God,
He will fill you with a joy that is not based on circumstance."

Father, I thank You when I am most empty,
there is more space for You to be present in my life.

6

SINGING IN THE PAIN
La-Tan Roland Murphy

I waited patiently for the LORD; He turned to me and heard my cry.
He lifted me out of the slimy pit, out of the mud and mire;
He set my feet on a rock and gave me a firm place to stand.
He put a new song in my mouth, a hymn of praise to our God.

—Psalm 40:1-3 (NIV)

"*Don't ever lose your song.*" I have been known to say this to friends and loved ones who were going through tough times. This quote holds a strong, unspoken message that says, "No matter what hardships you face in this life, a song will lift you up out of the pit and keep your heart encouraged!"

It's one thing to watch others go through financial crisis, yet it's another to go through it personally. I must confess, if this season of our lives was a test, I had failed terribly.

My faith had been so strong in years past—at least I thought so. In fact, I found great joy in testifying how God would provide for others in tough times. I repeatedly referred back to my parents'

story of financial despair, in an attempt to encourage others with
an eye-witness account. I shared how they persevered through the
toughest financial times. I became emotional while sharing the
heart-wrenching story about the loss of their home, land, and all
they had worked for as they prepared for retirement. Although
sharing such personal pain forced me to relive those days and
once again feel the sting of their devastating loss, I pushed myself
past my own raw emotions with self-surrendering determination
to share how God—the great Jehovah-Jireh—had proven Himself
faithful to provide.

Though I seemed strong while sharing *their* story, nothing
could have prepared me for what was ahead in my own life.
Financial despair, brought on by my husband's career change
and the insecurities that tagged along behind it, unveiled the
fullness of my frail humanity as I often wept into my pillow at
night. *Where was God in all of this? Had I been a silly optimist for
believing He would always come through?* The enemy rushed in
each morning, eager to fill my vulnerable ears with lies. He told
me I had been such a fool for boasting of my God's provisional
power. Although my heart knew better, my head warred against
the truth, and the lies often became my reality. All I could see was
doom and gloom. My heart lost its song.

Going from a six-figure income to a four-digit income
overnight tested our once unshakeable faith. My family's thriving,
comfortable, little world suddenly withered before our very eyes.
We felt trapped in a bad dream we couldn't wake up from. How
could we make it on a four-figure yearly income?

When my husband gave me the news of our financial situation, sheer panic grabbed me by my jugular. The faces of our three children drew close in my mind as fear gripped my once faith-filled heart with questions and concerns for how this could affect their immediate future.

Our oldest son would be going to college soon. We were even more distraught when the financial aid report came back showing he would get no financial assistance. Disbelief met despair as our eyes scanned the paperwork. *Surely, the loan company took note of the fact we were now only making a four-digit income!* Discouragement flooded every pocket of our weary hearts as we realized the loan company had based this decision on the six-figure income we earned the previous year.

To make things worse, my husband's mother, who had fought a fourteen-year-long battle with cancer, had been told by the doctors that the end was near. My father also lay bed-bound for two and a half years due to Parkinson's disease and cancer. The added stress of watching our loved ones suffer seemed too much to bear in itself. Now, we not only faced the loss of two spiritual giants we loved deeply, but we also faced the death of our financial hopes and dreams. Though not physically bed-bound like my sweet father, we realized we were bound to external realities that threatened to paralyze us as well. Though not physically sick, we were heartsick. We had lost our song.

My husband's parents lived three and a half hours away from us. Because we were in need of income—fast—my husband moved in with his parents. He'd help with the family business, since his mother was no longer able to work due to her increasing battle with cancer. After handling multi-million dollar corporate accounts in the business world, he became a used car salesman. Though we were thankful for God's provision, this shift in positions was a blow to his self-esteem as a man and as the head of our home. He had only worked in the field of telecommunications up to this point and had fully invested himself as a professional. He took pride in his work and in his ability to provide for our family. Though there were days I felt paralyzed by fear, my heart also felt sad for my husband. He faced so much change and loss after all those years of hard work, only to be forced to move in with his dear parents so we wouldn't have to uproot our children— especially our graduating senior. All of those things tore away at my husband's heart, but his audacious, determined spirit would not allow him to give up.

The weeks were long for me while I stayed in Raleigh to keep our home life going. The overwhelming responsibility of making sure our three children kept up in school, completed their homework, and followed through on all the extra-curricular activities, along with loneliness brought on by my husband's absence in our home, mingled with gut-wrenching grief for our dear parents' suffering.

Having a praise-filled attitude had been easy for me until going through this tough time. In fact, my friends and family often teased me about wearing rose-colored glasses, asking how I could see the good, even in the bad times in life. Now, the view from my world turned into a dizzying kaleidoscope of pain as my rose-colored life, defined by comfort and financial peace, went haywire.

Every prayer I prayed during this dark time seemed empty and powerless. Life felt different. I wanted things to be the way they used to be. I even expressed to a friend how strange I felt inside—like someone flipped a switch and my joy had been turned off.

I remember standing in front of the mirror staring blankly at a woman who looked like me. The financially comfortable version of me had a smile on her face. She felt safe and secure. She felt confident her financial needs would be met each day, as well as the needs of her children. Now I stood motionless and lifeless, and the blank look in my eyes said it all. *What happened to me, the woman who prided herself in singing her way through just about any difficult situation? What happened to my carefree spirit? What happened to my optimistic ability to "fake it until I could feel it?"* I could always muster up enough energy to deal with whatever "it" was. Although my heart had always had a song, there was no song of praise to be found anywhere near the pitiful, empty recesses of my soul. I felt shallow and guilty.

Though the circumstances surrounding my feelings would not quickly change, the woman in the mirror abruptly reminded me that I had to change. With my emotions ruled by our financial devastation and my joyful song interrupted, I could not sing through the pain. Though I knew God's word promised to take care of His children's needs according to His great riches in Christ Jesus, I had entered into a time of despair based on external things. The enemy took advantage, sneaking through the back door of my broken heart, like a robber in the night, and he took my most valuable source of strength—my joy.

I read in Nehemiah 8:10, *Go and enjoy choice food and sweet drinks, and send some to those who have nothing prepared. This day is holy to our Lord. Do not grieve, for the joy of the Lord is your strength.* No wonder I felt like I had concrete bricks strapped to my ankles. I had lost my joy. Because of that, I had lost my strength.

Could I muster up a song? Could I sing in the pain? Questions like these taunted my once optimistic heart. *Where was the song I prided myself in singing over others when they were going through struggles?*

In desperation, I asked the Lord to help me focus on everything praiseworthy in our lives. I was amazed by how many things He brought to mind. I began to thank God for all He had done for us in the past and for how faithful He had always been in supplying our every need. I asked Him to forgive my unbelief and fill me with a new joy that was not based on circumstances but on His power.

Though my circumstances didn't change overnight, God began to change me. He changed my perspective from loss to gain. He began to lift the veil that blocked my joy and allowed me to catch a glimpse of His heavenly perspective. He showed me how my husband's absence from our home allowed him to spend time with his mother in the last year of her life. Additionally, our trying circumstances gave our oldest son an opportunity to develop leadership skills before going out into the world, as he took on many of my husband's responsibilities. The Lord also established our marriage on a firmer foundation; we became much more of a team. Many weekends, when my husband came home, I had to go to Georgia to be with my ailing father. We could identify with each other's pain on a deep and personal level and support one another with compassion.

I still find myself amazed by the power of God and how He wastes nothing. When we surrender our deepest pain to Him, he takes it and molds it into something useful for His glory, giving us a powerful story to share with others who are going through tough times.

My husband and I have much more peace when we think of our future, because the Lord provided for us in miraculous ways. The part that left the deepest imprint in our hearts is how God provided not only for our physical needs, but He also provided for our emotional needs. To this day, we stand amazed at how gentle and tender-hearted He is toward His children. He sees each of us, knows us by name, loves us with an everlasting love, and provides for all our needs. He is ever-faithful and ever-true. He does not sleep while we struggle. He is always working for the good of those who put their hope and trust in Him. He gives power to the powerless, hope to the hopeless, joy to the joyless, and strength to the weak. He longs to put a new song in the hearts of his children who have lost their own in the midst of tough times.

Though your circumstances may not change, allow God to change your thinking. He has a good plan in mind for you and your family. Trust His heart and rest in knowing He is at work for you. Before you know it, you may find yourself singing in the pain.

Time to Reflect on God's Provision

God uses others to speak hope into us
when we are most hopeless.

*But encourage one another daily, as long as it is called Today,
so that none of you may be hardened by sin's deceitfulness.*
—Hebrews 3:13 (NIV)

BELIEVING GOD

Alycia W. Morales

For as the rain comes down ... and bring[s] forth and bud[s],
That it may give seed to the sower
And bread to the eater,
So shall My word be that goes forth from My mouth;
It shall not return to Me void,
But it shall accomplish what I please,
And it shall prosper in the thing for which I sent it.

—Isaiah 55:10-11 (NKJV)

My husband Victor looked uneasy after Pastor and Nan left our home late one July evening. We'd agreed, with witnesses, that I would resign my position as data entry specialist at CitiHope International so that I could stay home and raise the children God would bless us with over the next six years. I beamed with excitement and expectancy as my husband frowned, overshadowed with hesitancy. To say it would be easy—financially or otherwise—would be a really bad joke.

In August of 1999—two months before our one-year anniversary—we added our firstborn to our family of three. My step-son was now big brother to a Morales. Two years later, we added our second son. Thirteen months after that, we added our only daughter. And, two years later, we added our fourth and final child, another son. At the same time our daughter was born, we bought our first home, a fixer-upper on Main Street, right across the road from our beloved church. Vic worked in construction as a union carpenter. We lived in Upstate New York, where the economy slouched, even when it didn't in the rest of the nation.

The first prophetic word came in 2001. As always, Vic and I waited in line as the man of God prayed over church member after church member, bringing a word straight from the Lord. Matthew 10:41 says, *He who receives a prophet in the name of a prophet shall receive a prophet's reward.* We accepted the word of the prophet, anticipating that his reward would come with it. As Vic and I stood at the altar for prayer, God promised my husband that he would see an increase in his income. "A company man," the prophet said. Steady income. Stability. Prosperity. And we believed them, because we believe God.

Vic made decent money. While he worked, we made ends meet comfortably. However, when the job ended or the winter season rolled around, unemployment cut our income in half. As we dug the Chrysler Town and Country van we'd been blessed with out from under the snow, we dug ourselves deeper into a financial hole. It seemed like every month we called the mortgage company with yet another excuse as to why we couldn't make the payment on time. I stressed over whether or not we'd have electricity or enough heating oil to see us through to the next paycheck. In January and February, our utility bills increased by hundreds of dollars. I cringed as I watched the oil prices climbing and our income dwindling. For eight years, we rode the financial roller coaster of union work. For eight years, we listened every time the men of God spoke prosperity over our lives.

More often than not, I wondered if I should get a part-time job or just go back to work—even though I knew I needed to stay home with our babies. After doing some research, I discovered that childcare alone would cost any paycheck I could bring in. So, I stayed home.

And I prayed. I worried. I begged God, reminding Him of His promises. I fully expected Him to come through—and soon. "Stability in our finances, Lord. You promised my husband a position in a company. You promised prosperity. You said Your children won't beg for bread. I'm tired of getting out of a hole only to be pushed back into it. I'm tired of the on-again, off-again of our finances. We need help, Lord. We can't seem to get ahead …"

Despite our circumstances, we remained faithful with our tithe. Somehow, God always provided for our needs. Friends from church blessed us with vehicles. Once, a couple from the home group Vic and I led blessed us with an unexpected monetary gift. I think I paid the electric bill with it. We always qualified for food stamps or WIC (Women, Infants and Children) checks when our qualification period came around. Our church ran a community assistance program, so I could shop at highly discounted prices. Some weeks we were lucky to eat pasta every night. Others, I wished a gallon of milk and a loaf of bread would show up on our front porch. Once in a great while, we'd have steak and potatoes. Multiple times, we borrowed money from my parents to pay the electric bill, promising to repay them when Vic found his next job.

Thankfully, my husband was never one to sit around and do nothing. Two weeks after a lay-off, he'd be on the phone or back out the door, tracking down another construction job to work.

In the winter of 2007-2008, the union hired him to work a nuclear power plant shutdown. Work had been particularly slow that year, and we were desperate. For ten years, I'd told him he could never work out of town. He had to come home every night. With a teenaged step-son and four knee-cap kids running me in dizzying circles, I needed his help. Not that day. That day, we needed an income. I told him to take the job that would take him away from home for three months.

During those months he worked, I cried, and we dug out of our latest financial pit. About a month after being laid off from that job, he was hired for another one. For three more months he worked, I cried, and we continued to dig. And, the stress found a way to dig into our family.

Vic had been in and out of town for half the year. I'd taken a full-time job at our local bank, working as a teller, while our kids attended our local Christian Academy and my sister or my step-son babysat for me in the afternoons. Having neither of his parents around to pay attention to him, my step-son wore thin. As I received phone calls saying his homework wasn't completed the night before and that he was slacking off in school, tensions grew. My husband didn't want me disciplining his son, but he wasn't there to call the shots, either. One afternoon, Zachary came home from school and wanted to go to a friend's house. He'd been to a friend's house the night before and hadn't turned in the homework he never completed. I did what any parent should do and told him he'd have to stay home for the evening and do his work. Breaking point. A very upset and disappointed teenager left our home that evening and would spend his last year of high school back at his mom's.

Meanwhile, Vic blamed me for his son's leaving. Little did we know that God was working in the midst of our trials and had a plan of restoration for all of us.

Vic returned home from the power plant within a couple of weeks of Zach's departure. For two weeks, we waited for the union to call. Vic filed, once again, for unemployment benefits. And we prayed.

As usual, Vic became antsy. It was the week before Memorial Day, and he decided to start making phone calls. He'd written down the names and numbers of some of the guys he'd worked with at the power plant. He told me he wanted to call them to see if they knew of anymore shut downs and asked if I could pull out the box I'd mailed to him while he was at the last job. His cell phone had been stolen, and I'd had to ship him the new one when it came to our house. I never opened it. I never added anything to it. I just repacked it and mailed it off.

He opened it, and none of the papers he thought he'd kept in there were in the box. However, there was one piece of paper in the box. It had the number of a supervisor he'd worked under *four years prior* scribbled across it. "How did this get in there?" Vic looked quizzically at me.

"I have no idea," I replied.

"I didn't take it with me to the plant."

"I filed it a long time ago. It should be in a folder in the cabinet." Chills crept up my entire body as we both looked at each other in wonder.

"I guess I'll try him." Vic dialed the phone. His supervisor from an IBM project asked if he could call him back.

It was Memorial Day weekend. Thursday, to be exact. 2008. We'd *just* received Vic's first unemployment check, and his final paycheck had been spent. I wasn't due to be paid for another week; my checks were bi-weekly. We had $400 in our pockets.

The phone rang.

Vic's eyes grew large as I watched him converse, and he looked at me with his hand over the receiver. "Can I be in Alabama on Tuesday?"

What could I say? It would take an act of faith and a miracle, but it was an answer to ten years of fervent prayer. God's promise was finally manifesting itself, and there was no denying His hand in it.

"Sure." I shrugged my shoulders and waited for him to get off the phone.

A national concrete construction company hired my husband as a rod man on a steel mill project in Alabama. A rod man is the guy on a survey team who holds the stick while the guy with the laser shoots at it and gets the measurement he needs. Overnight, my husband went from working with his tools and brawn to working with his brain.

I began thanking God for His provision. My Jehovah-Jireh. I also began praying for Vic to have favor, not only with God, but with the men who'd hired him.

Within one month of being hired, Vic was promoted to gunman and given a salary, a living expense, a monthly plane ticket home, and a full benefit package. Within a few months, he was promoted to Lead Field Engineer. Guys had worked several years to get where God placed him in a matter of a moment.

For years, we had prayed and trusted God for my husband's overnight success. Since that fateful day in May 2008, the kids and I have joined their father on the adventure of a lifetime. We don't know when or where we're going next until an average of two weeks prior to our move. We move once every two years or so. God provides the finances we need every time. We no longer dig out of holes. We have more than enough. We're conquering the debts we could never touch before, like my college loans. God has remained faithful and true to His word.

My step-son's move back to his mother's house proved to be the best thing for all of us. He was able to finish out his senior year of high school with his friends, and we were able to travel without guilt. Knowing he was safe and secure gave us the peace we needed in our relationships. All continues to be well in our blended family dynamic. God had a plan, even in the midst of turmoil.

Some days may seem glum. God's promises may appear like they're sitting on the horizon, and every time you take a step toward them it may seem they sink below it once again. His word promises us that what He speaks over our lives will never come back void. These are the times to pray fervently and trust that He knows when the timing is perfect. The economy tanked just after we left our home and families behind to join God in the journey He called us to. It is with thanksgiving and faithfulness that we face each new day with Him.

Time to Reflect on God's Provision

The good thing about being broke is that we become
more sensitive to others in need.

Once I was young, and now I am old.
Yet I have never seen the godly abandoned or
their children begging for bread.

—Psalm 37:25 (NLT)

8

YOU CAN'T OUTGIVE GOD

Cynthia Howerter

"Bring the full tithe into the storehouse,
that there may be food in My house.
And thereby put Me to the test,"
says the Lord of hosts,
"see if I will not open the windows of heaven for you
and pour down for you a blessing until there is no more need."
—Malachi 3:10 (ESV)

When I was six years old, I accompanied my grandparents to a neighbor's ninetieth birthday party. I joined Mr. Bailey on his porch swing, and he pulled a coin out of his pocket. "Cynthia, this nickel is all the money I have left in this world. I don't need it because God gives me all I need." He placed the old Buffalo nickel in my palm. "I want you to have this. Never spend it. Whenever you look at it, remember that even if you give away your last nickel, you can't outgive God. Obey Him and He will always take care of you."

When my husband lost his job, he was given two months of severance pay. While we were very grateful for the short-term income, it didn't take long for those two months to go by, especially with two kids in college. I had never returned to work after giving up my teaching career—years before—when our first child was born, so our only income was from Tim's job. After several months of unemployment, I noticed Tim wasn't himself. A naturally upbeat man, he was somber and spoke little. Several days passed, but he still hadn't perked up.

"Tim, I can tell something's bothering you. What is it?"

He looked at the floor and took a slow breath. Exhaling, he lifted his head and looked at me. "We're going to run out of cash next week. After Tuesday, when I pay the mortgage and utilities, we won't have any money left. We won't even be able to buy milk."

I felt faint. "Nothing? Are you saying we'll be broke once you pay those bills?"

"Yes. I don't know what to do. We've never been in this situation."

I gripped the back of a chair while his words sunk in. "Well," I spoke slowly, "it sounds like our back is completely against the wall."

Tim nodded solemnly, his eyes not leaving mine. "I've known for a while, but I kept hoping I'd get a job before I had to tell you."

"It seems to me that we have only one recourse: we need to pray. God's our only hope."

"Can you pray, Cynthia? I'm not thinking clearly right now."

We held hands and bowed our heads. "Lord, our back is so firmly against the wall that the only way out is through You. In a few days, we'll be completely out of cash. We're facing disaster. Tim and I know that you are fully aware of our situation, and that only You can help us. So, Lord, we're asking You to help us in whatever way You know best. We thank You in advance for the good You'll do through this situation. Amen."

I lifted my head and looked into Tim's eyes. "We've done everything we can do with that prayer."

He nodded. "I'm going back upstairs to make some more calls. What are you going to do?"

"Laundry, some dusting, and I'll be praying—without ceasing. Don't worry, Tim. God knows our situation. We just need to trust Him to help us."

The next morning, our phone rang. It was my attorney calling to talk about my late-grandfather's trust, which couldn't be settled until certain conditions were met. Seventeen years had passed without the fulfillment of all terms. Over the years, Tim and I speculated about the reasons that prevented the trust from being settled, only to conclude that God had His own plan for it. And we knew, without question, that His motives were perfect—even if we didn't understand them.

To my surprise, my attorney told me that all of the conditions of the trust had finally been met. After hanging up, I turned and faced my husband.

"That was James. The conditions of Grandpa's trust have been met. He just put a check in the mail for us. We should get it in a day or two." Tim's jaw dropped. "It's enough for us to live on for a long time if we're frugal."

"This is the work of the Lord!" Tim bowed his head. "Lord, thank You. Thank You. Only You could have provided this money." Looking up, his face brightened and he smiled. "Cynthia, do you know what this means?"

"What?"

"Do you remember how we speculated for years about why the trust conditions weren't being met?"

"Yes."

"I understand now."

"You do?"

"Yes! It's because God knew all those years ago that we'd be in this financial predicament today, and He delayed the trust's settlement so He could provide the money at the exact time we needed it."

"Oh, my gosh. You're right! God knew all about this." I dropped into the chair I'd been holding onto. "Tim, I have something to say. I know this is the only money we'll most likely have until you get another job, but I feel very strongly that we need to tithe 10 percent of the inheritance check. God just blessed us and we need to be obedient and tithe."

Tim nodded. "I agree. Who should we give the money to?"

"I don't know. I'll pray and ask God to tell us."

Everything a person has is a gift from the Lord. A tithe, which is 10 percent, is only a portion of what God has already given to us. So when we tithe, we are actually returning a small portion to God. Tim and I understood that we would be tithing thousands of dollars when we had no current income and no assurance of employment. We also realized that we would be able to keep 90 percent, which was still a lot of money.

I asked God to tell me who He wanted the money to be distributed to. Names of individuals and organizations came instantly to me, and I wrote them all down. When I heard no more names, I asked God to tell me the amount of money that He wanted each to receive, and then I tallied the numbers. Twice. But the total didn't come to 10 percent—it went over by $125. For a moment, I pondered what I should do. An incredible peace came over me, and I realized that I could never outgive God. Hadn't He just given us enough money to live on for a long time? The reason God tells us to tithe from our increase is so He can bless us even more.

A relative chastised us for "giving away" 10 percent of my inheritance at a time of financial insecurity. "Don't you realize that there won't be any more money coming in until Tim finds a job?" Because Tim and I understood that it's always more important to obey God, I knew our decision to tithe was right with the Lord.

Once the inheritance check cleared the bank, I wrote and distributed checks to the people and organizations that God designated. One by one, each of the individuals called and asked how I knew they were having financial difficulties. There was no way I could have known, because they never told me. But God knew, and He provided for them through my obedience to Him. Tim and I were in awe at how God used the inheritance I had waited nearly two decades to receive in order to bless many.

We sold our house and after settlement at the end of April, we moved in with Aunt Emma, who lived halfway across the state. In June, my attorney called and told me that he'd just put a second check from my grandfather's trust in the mail. This time, the check was double the first one. God tells us in Malachi 3:10 to bring our tithes to Him and that if we are obedient, He will open the windows of heaven and pour out for us such blessing that there will not be room enough to receive it. Tim and I were overwhelmed by God's generosity, and we knelt as we tearfully thanked Him for His provision.

This time, Tim and I didn't need to discuss tithing. Looking into each other's eyes, we knew that we were going to give 10 percent back to the Lord. All we needed to do was ask God who He wanted to bless with this money. Once again, God provided the names of recipients. The joy that Tim and I felt at being able to help others in the midst of our own adversity was indescribable. Only God can take two people who have no jobs, no income, no money in the bank, no unemployment benefits, and no home of their own and give them thousands of dollars so they can provide for others in need.

About a month into our stay at Aunt Emma's house, the idea came to me that this time of unemployment would be a perfect time for Tim to pursue some necessary dental care which had been impossible with his demanding job schedule and the time-intensive nature of these dental procedures. I'd heard that dental schools charged reduced prices to patients. Our son's girlfriend, Sara,* was a dental student, so I called her and asked if Tim could be her patient. She said that he could and set up an appointment for Tim to be evaluated.

Sara and her professor thoroughly examined Tim and determined that the treatment he needed was far more extensive and costly than we'd guessed. Our mood on the drive home was somber. Even with the dental school's reduced price, we couldn't afford it. Once again, we turned to the Lord in prayer.

About a week later, Tim unexpectedly received a check in the mail from a long-dormant investment that we had written off as a total loss. The amount covered the entire cost of the dental bill. Keeping 90 percent for Tim's dental work, we tithed 10 percent and several more fortunate people received money they needed.

During our twenty-one months of unemployment, God provided all of our income through the long-awaited inheritance from my grandfather's trust and a resuscitated investment. Because both of our children were in college, we had ongoing expenses, but thanks to God's provision, we never missed or were late paying one single bill. We were able to pay the relative we lived with for our share of the utilities and food, and we kept our two cars operating. We paid for my attendance at two writers' conferences that supported my writing aspirations and created a potential new income source. And many people with financial needs were the recipients of our tithing money, which was incredible to us.

My husband was wrong when he told me that we'd be broke in a few days. You see, I still had Mr. Bailey's Buffalo nickel, and his words of wisdom were tucked firmly into my heart. When my husband and I obediently tithed thousands of dollars with no promise of receiving another cent, we learned that when we obey God, He assumes full responsibility and provision for all of our needs. No matter what your circumstances, you can never outgive God.

Name has been changed.

TIME TO REFLECT ON GOD'S PROVISION

We are so blessed, Father, to have access to Your holy word on a daily basis. May we always be good stewards of its teaching as we strive to *live* it to the fullest.

All Scripture is God-breathed and is useful for teaching, rebuking, correcting and training in righteousness.
—2 Timothy 3:16 (NIV)

2

GOD OF ALL THE YEARS
Cecil Stokes

For His anger endureth but a moment,
in His favour is life;
Weeping may endure for a night,
But joy cometh in the morning.

–Psalm 30:5 (KJV)

Several years ago, a good friend of mine introduced me to the concept of choosing a "word for the year." She asked God to give her a word that she could use as a mirror to see if the events of the year reflected what He had told her.

Her idea sounded great to me. I prayed and asked God for my word for the year, and I clearly heard Him say, "Jump." That's a fun first word. Since I'm a movie and television producer, I am constantly planning, and spontaneous is an ugly word to me. I interpreted jump to be the antithesis of planning. I vowed to say yes to as many offers as I was extended that year, to experience things I had never experienced, to jump at opportunities. What followed was one of the most memorable years of my life. I sailed on two cruises, fed stingrays out of my hand, built an eco-lodge in the Amazon, and hiked Machu Picchu. In previous years, I wouldn't have allowed myself to enjoy these things, because they would have taken me away from work for too long. I wouldn't have been as available for new projects. And honestly, I didn't think I deserved that much fun. In the year of jump, I also broke my foot and wrecked my car. Sweet memories indeed. Yes, I am being serious.

I eagerly awaited my next word for the year. About two weeks before New Year's, I began to pray for it and pretty quickly heard God say, "Risk." Being a producer, I constantly negotiate, so I immediately began to persuade God that "Peace" would be a much better word for the year. Ha ha. My attempt didn't work; risk was the new word of the year.

In my career as a freelancer, I always have about a dozen projects in development and can rarely see more than a few months in advance of the work coming my way. Toward the end of the year of jump, I had taken an actual job. It was a phenomenal opportunity in entertainment, and when I prayed, the job was exactly where God wanted me and what He wanted me to do. Little did I know that risk was heading my way. Because of the full-time nature of the new job, I stopped juggling multiple projects and focused on just a few. And, soon after the year of risk began, I was miserable. I missed the freedom of freelancing and getting to switch from one project to another seemingly on a whim. I began developing a new film with an old friend who ended up betraying me. Because of my new busyness, I had willingly severed ties to some good freelance work.

By the spring of the year of risk, I begged God to release me from the new job I had, but because He had directed me to take the job, I wouldn't resign until He allowed me to leave. I worked so much, I neglected and ignored friendships. I cut myself off from my own life. I sequestered myself out of misery. I daily bargained with God, offering up the comforts of my life in exchange for being released from this job. I told Him I didn't care if I lost my house, lost my car ... nothing mattered to me if He would only allow me to quit. For months, He said no. I was getting desperate, but I continued working that job to the best of my abilities. After almost four months of begging for release, He finally gave it. I was free, back to my old life. But to my dismay, much of my old life did not remain.

As a freelancer, I had saved a good amount of money to hold me over for the time in between gigs, but because I'd severed most of my freelancing ties, the money dwindled toward the end of the year of risk. I still reeled from the betrayal of not just one, but two friends who I had begun projects with, and I believe I was in a state of shock from all I had gone through with the job. I diligently sought new work, but none could be found. I made contacts for gigs far beneath my experience level, and I didn't even get those. Money became very tight. I vividly remember thinking one day, "Is deodorant really a necessity or just a luxury?" Each month, I searched my house for items to sell on eBay and Craigslist just to scrape by. I fell behind on my mortgage by several months, and

I didn't know where I'd soon be living. By the way, it turns out deodorant was a necessity.

I couldn't believe what was happening to me. I had won every award that existed in my field, and I could not find work. Had I left my previous job too soon? No, I didn't regret that decision; I was even more miserable at that job with money than now, without.

And do you know what happens when someone who loves to stay busy doesn't have work for prolonged periods of time? I began to over-think everything. I didn't allow myself to rebuild neglected relationships, because I identified my self-worth with my career, with what I did for a living. I was in self-inflicted exile with no foreseeable projects. Times got very tough. I sold my car. Since it was paid for, it provided money for a few more months. I was now so many payments behind on my mortgage that I feared foreclosure. I met with a realtor to see if I had any options. Of course under the guise of, "I never know where work will take me, so I need to stay fluid ..." When you have almost nothing left, how does pride remain? Things got so bad I began checking into work at minimum wage establishments. There is nothing wrong with those jobs, but I thought I had put in my time when I was younger. Then, something beautiful happened.

I prayed more than I'd ever prayed in my life. And I stayed silent so I could actually hear God's voice. I humbled myself before God. I wanted to show Him in a tangible way how I felt about Him—totally dependent. When I would awake in the morning, I rolled out of my bed and directly onto my knees (never allowing my feet to touch the floor). I could no longer stand on my own two feet, and I wanted to show Him that I knew that. If the thought ever crossed my mind to kneel before Him, I did so, and in the strangest of places. But I wouldn't allow the thought to cross my mind to bow without being obedient. I no longer had anything to give except myself. One morning I bowed before God, begging for His provision, and I began to sob (more so than possibly ever before). I lay down on the carpet, face to the floor, and cried with deep guttural sobs reserved only for death. I asked Him to give me work that He saw fit for me. It didn't have to be up to my standards, just what He wanted me to do. I told Him I had nothing left but Him, and I would do whatever He asked.

Never in my life of following God had I allowed Him to be my all. I'd always credited Him with what I'd accomplished, and I truly knew I could do nothing without Him. But, I believed I was responsible for how I used the gifts He had given me. It was only when absolutely nothing remained that I actually became what He created me to be—fully dependent on Him. In that moment and in the following days, I came to truly understand for the very first time in my life that God is my protector, my healer, and my provider. He supplies all.

I had learned my lesson. But my circumstances did not change. New projects did not suddenly drop from the sky. My money worries did not end. I didn't understand. I finally realized where my income truly came from, but it did not magically start flowing again. I was perplexed. "I understand, God. I see what You have taught me. You can end this lesson now and allow me to move on," I prayed. But my circumstances did not change.

A new year approached, and I was more than ready to replace the word risk. I prayed for my next word for the year, and I was thrilled to hear "Reward." God told me risk will always be followed by reward. Folks, I'm human. I thought I knew exactly what reward meant: riches. I would be paid back ten-fold for what I had lost. This would be the year one of my projects would hit big. I would probably become a millionaire in my year of reward. But month by month, riches did not come. However, God did provide. While I was still so behind, He did supply what I needed to get by. A check from a law firm for incorrect closing costs five years before, small projects that paid more than they should have, writing conferences and film festivals that popped up out of the blue. A small independent film that I would have never had time to make if I had real jobs coming in ... But still no millions.

As the year of reward came to a close, I looked back, wondering what God had meant by His word choice for the year. And again, I wound up face-down on the carpet and sobbing, but this time they were intense sobs of life. He revealed what I had gained that year.

After four years of church hopping, I had finally taken the time to find a church home. The fellowship of believers who quickly became dear friends filled parts of me I didn't know were empty. They didn't know who I thought I was. They just loved me for who I am. And the best friend I have ever had in my life? I met him through that job from which I had begged to be released. We met two months after I petitioned God to allow me to quit. God had many reasons to keep me there just a little longer, and

I was beginning to understand why. I won't question His timing anymore.

The year of reward ended, and I embraced my word for the next year: "Fly." Soar as only you can soar when God lifts you up. Rise above as you only can when He is your foundation. If you let Him carry you, your feet never have to touch the ground. And that little independent film I could have never been a part of in my old life? It was called *OCTOBER BABY*—the first major theater release of my career—and a movie that would change not just my life, but create life-long ripples in the lives of thousands who viewed it.

Time to Reflect on God's Provision

"What do you mean we have no health insurance?"

Lord, You are the great physician.
From the beginning to the end of my days,
I will put my trust in You.

10

HE MAKES ALL THINGS NEW
La-Tan Roland Murphy

He who was seated on the throne said,
"I am making everything new!"
Then he said, "Write this down, for these words
are trustworthy and true."

—Revelation 21:5 (NIV)

Spring was in full bloom. The small dogwood tree outside my office window, the azalea bushes bursting forth with beautiful shades of fuchsia, the delicate roses I'd planted by the mailbox, and the lush lawn filling the air with the scent of freshly cut grass—all sent forth their joyful signals that spring was finally here.

My husband and I needed something fresh and new. I eagerly hung my beloved spring flag, beautifully stitched with hydrangea blooms, on the pole above the porch steps. The winter months had seemed much colder than winters past. Perhaps it was because we felt the harsh winds of financial change blowing in our lives as we faced the bitter reality of investments gone bad.

This was a season in life when we should have been ready for retirement, while feeling a sense of financial freedom, a result of our hard work through the years. The financial weather report at this time in our lives should have read: *Financially Secure/Retirement Ready,* but that was not the weather report at the Murphy home. Instead, like an unexpected ice storm in the middle of spring, we suddenly found ourselves in a financial freeze-out.

My husband had been invited by a colleague to invest in a business that seemed too good to pass up—a cutting-edge adventure. He welcomed the challenge this partnership would bring and longed to be back in his field—computer technology. Although the car sales position he held in the family business for almost a year had literally been our financial life-line, my husband felt confident it was time for him to move back into his area of expertise.

It has been said that "if a person does not take risks in life, they will never succeed." With that thought in mind, we invested everything we'd saved in order to launch the new business endeavor. Our hopes flew as high as a kite in a springtime breeze. This was a welcomed feeling, because we'd been trapped in a five-year financial storm that seemed like a long, cruel winter.

The first year of our new investment adventure seemed promising. The second year, we were still hopeful that once we got past the initial investment expenses, we'd turn a profit and recover the monies we'd originally invested. We were excited and anxious, hoping to glean a bountiful harvest from our financial seed-sowing endeavor. By the third year, the profit numbers declined as the company expanded for future growth.

During these years, we struggled to keep our faith. We had taken the risk and still felt confident that the fruit of our harvest was coming. Life was stressful, and the fight for our joy was brutal in this cold season. We were thankful that our hope was grounded in eternal things. After witnessing first-hand the suffering of loved ones as they passed from this world into the heavenly realm, we realized our financial battles paled in comparison. This truth, ever-present in our hearts and minds, kept us going forward in hope and not despair. Although we still felt trapped in our financial winter, we understood that spring would come if we persevered.

I cannot mislead you into thinking we kept our "springtime hope" on a daily basis. At times, facing even one day was overwhelming. But the Lord, in His sweetness, taught us to be patient and live in Him moment by moment, one faithful breath at a time. He reminded us through His word that He foresaw this season of our lives from the cross, where He willingly died, and that He died to take on the sting of this painful season—all for us.

Like the beautiful blooms I watched from my office window, we longed for the beauty of feeling alive again. The Lord gently reminded us that He died so that we might have a full life in Him. He longs for His children to have true freedom in every season of life—spiritually, physically, and financially. It was clear to us that we were *not* free. We longed for the freedom Christ had in mind for those who would put their hope and trust in Him. Not in part, but the whole.

The time had come for us to get out of the business partnership. We were ready to walk away from our bad investment. What appeared to be a winter wonderland proved to be an avalanche— one that threatened to wipe us out financially if we didn't move toward the exit sign. We couldn't help but wonder if we had stepped into this business endeavor without seeking the wisdom of God. From the start, it had not been blessed.

The financial stress kept mounting, although the company began to turn great profits. My husband hadn't taken a salary from the company for some time now. One year, we were only able to take $8,000 from the business as income, and another year, we were unable to take any salary. The stack of bills piled higher and higher as each day passed. Our savings dwindled down to nothing. We worried how we would provide for our family of five on such little income.

From an accounting standpoint, one would think this was a successful and viable business that brought in enough for us to live comfortably. But the outflow of cash was more than the inflow. The need to hire other employees and purchase more efficient equipment, along with general office expenses, left little in the checkbook to pay the owners. Because we owned 40 percent of the company, we were responsible to pay taxes on that percentage. According to accounting practices, it *was* a profit. We had no idea where the tax money would come from since this was the year we had taken no salary for ourselves. Once again, bitter financial winds blew across our frost-bitten hearts. Nothing could have prepared us for this. We were exhausted, both emotionally and physically.

One day, when I felt exceptionally helpless, I had a flashback to 1999, when we had twenty-four inches of snowfall in our area. Our Lhasa Apso puppy loved playing in the snow with the children, but being so small, it swallowed her up. When her head came out of the snow, her eyes and nose were the only exposed parts of her. We laughed at her audacious spirit and determination. Right before she ran off into a deep, snow-filled ditch, we rescued her. We bundled her in a towel and took her inside where she could be warm and safe. This situation was much too big for her.

While reminiscing over a warm cup of coffee, I realized the financial snowstorm we faced was much too big for us. Our hearts cried out for someone to rescue us. My husband and I desperately wanted to be in a different season.

Another harsh financial wind blew our way the day we received notification that we owed the government an overwhelming amount of taxes. With no money to pay them, we were in a state of shock and disbelief that this was happening. A dear friend sent me an email one day, saying she had been researching some things online and came across a website saying there was unclaimed money out there, and our names were on the list. Desperation overshadowed any thought that this could be a scam. My husband did his own research and found that our names were indeed on the list. He inquired about the money and found that a company he had worked for twenty years earlier owed us thousands of dollars. Our hearts rejoiced, because we knew it was the Lord's way of lifting us up out of the bitter snow, wrapping us in a towel, and taking us out of the cold. God knew this situation was too big for my husband and me, and He had not overlooked our need. When the check arrived, it was only a few dollars off from being the exact amount we needed to pay the government the taxes we owed.

It was a miracle! We were in awe that the awesome God of the universe came to our rescue. The freedom we felt when we could pay our taxes was indescribable. Our springtime had finally arrived. Our joy for God's provision felt like the sun was shining in our hearts; the dogwood trees were in full bloom, and the fuchsia azaleas burst forth with color. We were thankful for the warm, gentle breeze of the Lord's power that had blown into our lives. We felt like God Himself had hung the springtime flag out by the front steps leading up to our hearts' door as He ushered in a new season of our lives.

Though there have been many more winter storm advisories seeking to rob us of our sweet springtime, it is through prayer that our decisions are based. My husband and I ask God to give us wisdom in all things, and He has been faithful to do so. His provisions are bountiful. His faithfulness never ends. In the most amazing and unexpected ways, He provides for those who put their hope and trust in Him.

Every season of life brings changes. But the true test of our faith is when old man winter comes for a visit bearing a knapsack filled with financial burdens. It is then that we discover how small we are and how big God is. It is then we are able to fully realize the power of His unfailing provision.

Although we are still recovering from the devastation that the long, icy winters of our lives have caused, our faith is stronger for having experienced this season. We have far to go in recovering from the aftermath of these storms. The retirement years tap us on the shoulder from time to time to remind us that time is of the essence. Still, there is a deep, settled peace in knowing that as long as we do our part and remain centered on God's unfailing guidance in all things, He will make all things new in His time, including us.

Time to Reflect on God's Provision

I thought I was chasing after the American Dream,
until I realized that the American Dream was chasing me.
I am broken now, Lord, and I need You to guide my way.

The Lord will guide you always;
He will satisfy your needs in a sun-scorched land
and will strengthen your frame.
You will be like a well-watered garden,
like a spring whose waters never fail.
Your people will rebuild the ancient ruins
and will raise up the age-old foundations;
you will be called Repairer of Broken Walls,
Restorer of Streets with Dwellings.

—Isaiah 58:11-12 (NIV)

11

TRUSTING GOD, NOT THE AMERICAN DREAM

Beth K. Fortune

Consider it pure joy, my brothers and sisters, whenever you face trials of many kinds, because you know that the testing of your faith produces perseverance.

—James 1:2-3 (NIV)

As I made my way to the back of the store, I knew I had timed my excursion right, for there in front of me I found what I was seeking—a cart, piled high with a variety of boxes. Some people know where to find the tastiest ice cream sundae, the best bargain on shoes, or the most unique pieces of art, but I had become quite the expert on finding the ever-so-important pieces of cardboard.

My husband's unemployment had landed us in a financial crisis, prompting yet another move. Frustration mounted within our family, because even though we had struggled before, money had never been this tight. Monthly paychecks were consumed within the first couple of weeks. Even with a part-time job at a garden center, the money lasted about as long as a good watering on a hot summer day. We'd already downsized from a three-bedroom home to a one bedroom, but we couldn't even afford the smaller home.

We faced the discouraging fact that we couldn't make it on our own any longer. The thought of asking our parents if we could live with them weighed heavily on us, but we realized we had no other choice. My in-laws had a four-room apartment in their basement, so we thought we would talk to them first. It was an emotional scene as my husband approached his parents and explained our situation and asked if we could move in with them. They both agreed, so we began packing. The magnet I always kept on my refrigerator that boldly pronounced "I always bloom where I'm planted" nudged me to keep some of our personal items while everything else headed to storage for an undetermined time.

This was the most difficult move to date. Usually a move offers a sense of excitement as one anticipates a new place, new surroundings, new ways to decorate, as well as new dreams. Feelings of defeat and discouragement replaced that excitement.

I was grateful to have a place to live and thankful my husband's parents allowed us to share their home. I wasn't concerned about how we'd get along because we had a good relationship with them. Each night, as I placed my head on my pillow, looking at the same walls my husband had seen as a growing boy, I asked God to help me with the worry about our future that spun its web around me.

While living at my in-laws', my husband received a call from our denomination's mission director telling him of an interim pastor opening. Being an ordained minister and having pastored churches in the past, this was an answer to a prayer to get back into the ministry and out of commission-only jobs. After preaching several times at the prospective church, we were not only welcomed with open arms, but we were offered the position. Not only did the church offer us the job, but they had a house for us. That night, I placed my head on my pillow, but instead of seeing the walls of my husband's childhood room, I saw our new home. The next day, I didn't let an opportunity go by without testifying about God's faithfulness, His goodness, and His provision. He'd not only found my husband a job, He'd found us a home. God had finally answered our prayer with not only a job, but a job in ministry.

With no warning, we received a phone call that brought back the feelings of defeat and discouragement. The church decided to call another pastor as interim and my husband would no longer be needed. After all we had been through, to come so close to a job and a beautiful home only to have both slip away … this was the worst. Now we had no job and were still living in my in-laws' basement.

I already questioned the idea of the American Dream, but now I questioned God. I knew the Scriptures warned that there would be trials and tribulations and that we would have burdens and would need to cast them upon an omnipotent Heavenly Father. Having served with my husband in ministry for the first half of our marriage, I still couldn't understand why God allowed this to happen. The only thing I was sure of was that I was more discouraged and now allowed worry and fear to rule my life.

As a dandelion slowly but deliberately breaks through a crack in the sidewalk, pride broke through the cracks of my Christian armor. I felt embarrassed for my friends and family to find out what we were going through. For those who did know, I felt I had to act as though I was strong and full of faith. Discontent came close alongside pride. I knew these were sin and I needed to trust God, but I couldn't see God in any of our circumstances.

After living with my in-laws for six months, we felt we needed to find our own place. Watching us, along with being splashed by the waves of our disappointment, was too much for his aging parents. No matter what, it was time to trust God to take care of us.

With no money in the bank, no money for a rental deposit, and no job for my husband, we took a big step of faith. While following a lead on a two-bedroom townhouse, we were introduced to a man who had recently lost his business and had to start over again. He understood our situation and offered us the townhouse with no up-front deposits and reduced rent until my husband found employment. Through this encounter, I realized that others also faced financial obstacles and were able to get back on their feet. A seed of hope settled in my heart, and I watered it with prayer and God's words. As one throws out rotting produce to make room for fresh produce, I threw out the negative thoughts that were my constant companion and replaced them with positive thoughts.

It didn't take long to move the possessions we had at my in-laws', along with some of our furniture and belongings from storage, into our new home. We took the step, moved in, and waited to see how God would provide.

Day after day, my husband continued searching for jobs. I spent my days holding my shoulders back and wearing a smile on my face. Only a few knew of the anguish and worry behind the facade.

To me, this was added pressure. I felt I needed to be a super Christian, always optimistic and joyful. I found out there was nothing super about my walk with the Lord. I was weak and untrusting and had very little joy. I woke up each morning trying my best to stay positive, but the proverbial silver lining in the cloud taunted me as I chased after it, watching it blow in the opposite direction. It was always there but out of reach.

My morning talks with God became more of a crying session that led to a pity party and sometimes into ugly temper tantrums. I would pray, but God was silent. In His silence, my heart's cry became, "Lord, just help me get through today."

Only with God's provisions did we make it through the first month. These came in many ways. My mom would slip me twenty dollars to help with gas. My husband's parents would fill a grocery bag with a roast, some bacon, and a loaf of bread. As difficult as it was, God began to work on the pride that had taken root in both mine and my husband's heart. With God's grace, we accepted help from family and friends. We saw a family member's offer to make a car payment as a provision that allowed us to buy groceries. The times when a friend treated me to lunch or my husband to a round of golf became a welcome reprieve from the stress.

These moments reminded me of all the instances in our past when we had given to others without expecting anything in return. As a couple, we found it much easier to be on the giving end than the receiving. Humility replaced our pride as we let God soften the parts of our hearts that the enemy tried to harden.

The second month living on our own, my husband was offered a management job and promised salary and commission, only to be informed a week later that it would be commission only. We wanted to give up but knew we had no choice but to keep praying and trusting God. My morning talks with God became a little more controlled, with less crying, but I still dealt with worry and fear. I continued to pray, but God was still silent. In His silence, my heart cried out, "Lord, just help me get through today."

A few weeks later, my husband received a job offer that included salary plus commission and health benefits. Our prayers for employment had been answered.

Even though the wolves were no longer at the door, they still circled in the front yard, waiting for a chance to steal from us. I knew it would take a while to get back on our feet financially, but I didn't realize how long. As we continued to walk through this difficult time, I had to dig deep and examine my heart. God's Word says, *Above all else, guard your heart, for everything you do flows from it* (Proverbs 4:23 NIV). Like a sponge that exudes whatever is inside of it when pressed, I too exuded what was in my heart when pressed. As the pressure mounted, I'd like to say I exuded joy, peace, patience, kindness, and long-suffering, but that wasn't the case.

I also had to examine who was on the throne of my life—God or me. Going through the seasons of unemployment and recovery have been difficult, but I've learned to let go and let God take charge. I've had to release the details, the disappointments, and especially the delusion that just because I'm a child of God, everything in my life is going to go as I think it should. I had to come to terms with the fact that the American Dream of large houses filled with the latest gadgets and gizmos and surrounded by white picket fences is only a dream, and I need to trust God in all things.

I'm learning, even though we still struggle, that God is in the center of it all. This world and everything it has to offer is only temporal. Understanding this important truth has helped me keep our trials and struggles in perspective. It's not easy, but I try to consider it joy as I live through these trials, because I realize this testing of my faith produces perseverance in me and my family.

Today, my morning talks with God are centered on Him, not me. My tears are no longer from anguish or pity parties but are the result of thanksgiving and praises for God's love. I sing as David did, *In you, Lord my God, I put my trust* (Psalm 25:1 NIV). When I pray, God's still silent. But in His silence my heart hears, *I'm here, Beth, and I will help you get through today.*

TIME TO REFLECT ON GOD'S PROVISION

From God's perspective, a job loss can be
a promotion in disguise.

Forget the former things, do not dwell on the past.
See, I am doing a new thing.
Now it springs up, do you not perceive it?

—Isaiah 43:18 (NIV)

12

UNRAVELING RELATIONSHIPS
Deborah Raney

I consider that our present sufferings
are not worth comparing with the glory that will be revealed in us.
For in this hope [Jesus] we were saved. But hope
that is seen is no hope at all.
Who hopes for what they already have?
But if we hope for what we do not yet have, we wait for it patiently.

—Romans 8:18, 24-25 (NIV)

There is nothing like a good financial crisis to create a parallel crisis in relationships. I think that was perhaps the most difficult thing my husband and I experienced when he was unexpectedly laid off from his job as an advertising manager after twenty-five years of faithful employment. At a time when we most needed the strength of relationships, it seemed they felt most fragile.

In our marriage, we disagreed (vehemently for a few months) about what the next step should be. My husband felt God was calling him to start a new business. To me that seemed just short of insane, given that the venture would cost money, not bring in money. Thankfully, after an agonizing day spent in prayer, fasting, and seeking God's will, I was finally able to come alongside Ken and support him in his venture. But it became clear right away that this "new normal" would mean a drastic lifestyle change for us.

We immediately sought ways to quit spending and get out from under any debts we could. This meant using part of our savings to pay off our credit cards and pay down our mortgage so we could stay in our home. It also meant, eventually, selling our second car—the one our youngest daughter drove to school. To her credit, she was very understanding about the need to cut back. But my husband and I both felt some guilt about the fact that our daughter had to give up so much for circumstances that were no fault of her own. (Looking back, we see that those sacrifices helped prepare her for being a poor college student and recently, a newlywed.)

In the early days of our crisis, our friends and family were very sympathetic of our situation and offered to help in many ways. Each of our parents offered financial help. We were grateful, yet, since we both come from large families, it seemed unfair to our siblings to accept that help.

Our grown children also offered encouragement, help, and hope—each in their own way. Our eldest daughter mailed us a box of oatmeal, a sweet reminder of our impoverished newlywed days when we once ate oatmeal three times a day for almost a week, knowing every bite was God's provision. It was a story we'd shared often with our kids, and we will never forget that symbol of hope our daughter offered us. To this day, that (now empty) Quaker oatmeal box sits on a shelf as a testament to God's very practical care for us.

Our eldest son helped by selling his old car to his little sister for a steal—and on a payment plan she could afford. Our youngest son and his wife, newlyweds with college loans to pay, offered us their sizable income tax refund. We were grateful we never found it necessary to take them up on the offer, but there was much comfort in knowing those funds were available if we had an emergency.

It was such a blessing to see our kids acknowledge our struggle and speak back to us our own belief in God's provision. Yet, while we were so grateful for their support, it was sometimes embarrassing and humbling to have to admit our financial need to those we felt should be depending on *us* for help.

Many friends offered help in ways that preserved our dignity— inviting us to share a meal and sending the leftovers home with us; cleaning out their cupboards and gifting us packages of coffee and shampoo and other staples they claimed they would never use. One of my sisters bought me several new outfits when my wardrobe needed a boost. And a couple of friends, knowing how much I love planting flowerpots each spring, gave me gift certificates to the garden store. It was a luxury I could never have afforded that year. Sometimes when friends or family bought me things, I felt guilty, as if accepting their gifts somehow dishonored my husband, whose "fault" it was that I could no longer afford nice things.

When we were pinching pennies so tightly just trying to pay our basic bills, I was often upset with friends who took lightly their ability to come up with the money to eat out or go to the movies—luxuries we could no longer afford. I wanted to lecture friends who complained about inconsequential problems when they had so many material possessions.

It stung to hear friends "brag" about their latest purchase or mention paying the amount of our meager monthly grocery bill for something I now deemed frivolous. It seemed terribly insensitive for people to speak so casually of their purchases when we were on a major spending freeze. Yet, when I learned that a close relative had thoughtfully "hidden" their purchase of a new vehicle from us, I felt hurt and left out, and I wondered what else people were keeping from us. Not normally an ultra-sensitive person, I suddenly felt angry and hurt much of the time. My poor friends couldn't win for losing!

We pray that our experience has made us more sensitive to others who might be going through similar trials. I'm sure that before this experience, I said thoughtless things to friends who were struggling financially or in other ways. Realizing that it was never my intention to be hurtful has helped me understand those who behaved insensitively toward us. I hope our ordeal has caused me to be more careful and thoughtful with my words and actions.

An unexpected relationship issue cropped up the first time we went to a public event in our small town and realized we might run into my husband's former bosses. Although my husband remained friends with the team he led at the company, we sometimes felt awkward around former coworkers who had dodged the layoff bullet. We both struggled with feelings of betrayal and bitterness, and early on we committed to pray for the families who ran the company.

I thought I was doing pretty well in the forgiveness department until the first encounter with someone responsible for Ken's layoff. I was surprised by the ugly emotions that surfaced, and I'm ashamed to say I fled without speaking to the person. (Though perhaps it's a good thing I didn't stick around to voice my opinions!) To this day, four years later, we pray together for my husband's former company and for the families involved. That small act truly has been the secret to healing that bitterness.

While God met every single physical need we had during this difficult period, He also provided richly for us through sermons, devotions, books, and songs we heard on the radio. At the time of Ken's layoff, our daughter was in a high school singing group, and we were scheduled to attend the various churches where the group was performing that winter. At first, it felt like a cruel joke that we would be attending an unfamiliar church the very first Sunday of our crisis. But God had something else in mind.

The usher who greeted us that morning was a man who'd been a victim of the same layoff. He was exactly the person Ken needed to see that morning. The sermon that day, and so many messages from various pulpits in the weeks to come, felt as if God spoke directly to us—words of comfort and healing and wisdom. Words that gave us hope that we had not been abandoned and that God still had a plan for our lives. A good plan.

Several friends suggested books and DVDs they thought would be helpful, and those, too, spoke to us and guided us through important and difficult decisions. One book, suggested by my sister after she heard the author speak on the radio, was *Plan B* by Pete Wilson. We ended up hosting a small group from our church and together we studied that book. We discovered that although the "Plan B" of others was different from ours, God allowed us to comfort and encourage one another.

So many of the friendships—and even minor acquaintances—that God established in our lives before Ken was laid off became richer and more meaningful in the aftermath. Again and again, God placed people in our path who offered pieces of the puzzle we were trying to put together. A woman from our church alerted us to a great mortgage loan rate her bank was offering. We were able to save thousands of dollars and knock years off our mortgage by refinancing.

Other friends steered people to Ken's new graphic design business or brought him work themselves. A friend with banking and accounting expertise offered to help Ken set up his business and prepared all the complicated tax documents—no charge.

There were more than a few who were skeptical about Ken's plans (including his wife, for a while!), but even those helped us to see angles we hadn't thought of before and to be better prepared as Ken launched his business.

The passing of time and a new direction in life—one in which we *both* clearly see God's hand—have eased nearly all the discomfort we felt in relationships during those early days. Even though we still must be extremely careful with our money, and retirement isn't something we dare to dream about yet, we look back on the amazing and even miraculous ways God provided for us during our financial crisis, and we know that we can trust Him with our future.

We've both declared that—given the choice—we would not for one minute wish away what happened. We are stronger people, more solid in our marriage, better friends, deeper in our faith, and closer to the Lord for having gone through this. Best of all, we see Romans 8:28 being played out in our lives daily. We are living proof that *all things* (not just the good things) *work together for good to those who love God and are called according to His purpose.* We are learning that being forced to live one day at a time has a tendency to keep our eyes focused on the Lord and makes us more mindful of His wonderful provision for His children.

Changing our mindset to view our circumstances as an adventure and a mission, rather than a hardship, has caused the most dramatic growth spurt in each of our journeys of faith since we first came to Christ as teenagers. We can hardly wait to see what God has in mind for our tomorrow!

TIME TO REFLECT ON GOD'S PROVISION

Oh, Lord, help us to walk away from our old life
—the things that once looked so wonderful—
and walk close to You.

*My grace is sufficient for you, for My power
is made perfect in weakness.*

—2 Corinthians 12:9 (NIV)

13

FACING FORWARD

Cynthia Howerter

I press on toward the goal to win the prize
for which God has called me heavenward in Christ Jesus.
—Philippians 3:14 (NIV)

Before I'd packed a single box, I walked through the rooms of our house. I realized that they were actually rooms of my life because of the memories they held, and I wondered how I could move away from the life my family and I had known. The Bible story of Lot's wife came to mind, and I understood my choices: either look behind at the past and be immobilized—or face forward and move on to God's best.

When we bought the house in Pittsburgh, our son, Justin, was in first grade and our daughter, Megan, was in pre-school. During the nineteen years we called the Dutch colonial home, we celebrated many birthdays, anniversaries, and milestones. I particularly loved its location on top of a steep hill with sweeping views of woodlands. Now, because of my husband's job loss, we were selling our house and preparing to leave. After years of living on top of our hill, my family and I faced a plunge into a valley of unknowns.

Each morning, after thanking God for the blessings He continued to give my family and me, I faced a day of decisions and packing—all the while wondering where we'd relocate if Tim got a job and where we'd go if he didn't. Working in one room at a time, I methodically sorted through closets and drawers, deciding what to keep and what to give up. Clothes that were outdated or didn't fit were donated to charity—those were easy decisions. Deciding what possessions to keep was more difficult. I used a guideline: if the item hadn't been used in the past five years, I donated it. The exceptions to this were family heirlooms and most of our furniture; those were kept. To keep my attitude positive, I told myself that our house needed to be de-cluttered and this was the opportunity to do it.

After many discussions and prayers, Tim and I developed a plan for our short-term future. If Tim got a job before we had to leave the house, our packed possessions meant that we could move easily and quickly. If he didn't find employment before settlement, we'd need to place our belongings in storage and find new housing.

As the time for settlement approached and no job materialized, Tim and I selected a moving company and set a date for them to take our possessions to their storage facility. Next, we turned our attention to finding an inexpensive place to live. When my Aunt Emma* offered to let Tim and me stay with her, we knew the Lord was providing a good solution. Because Justin and Megan were still in graduate schools, they would remain in their apartments.

With our plans in place, Tim continued job hunting while I packed. Before we knew it, Easter weekend arrived—two weeks before the movers were scheduled. Megan and Justin came home from school, and we loaded their cars with the few remaining possessions in their bedrooms.

Sitting down to Easter dinner—our last meal together in our house—was one of the most difficult things our family has ever done. The temptation we faced was to focus on our current situation.

As we sat around the table, the four of us formed a circle by holding hands, and Tim began the prayer. "Lord, we're grateful for this Easter Sunday and our risen Lord. We thank You for the many years our family has spent in this beautiful house—the house You gave us. Please be with our family as we leave our home."

Weeping interrupted Tim's prayer. Justin pushed his dinner plate to the center of the table and laid his head upon his arms. His body shook with emotion.

"Stop, Tim. Just say amen." My voice quivered.

Pushing her chair away from the table, Megan ran upstairs to her room.

"But I'm praying for us."

"We can't pray right now. We're in too much pain."

Lifting his head, Justin whispered, "I can't eat." He left the table and ran upstairs to his room.

"I'm so sorry." Tears dripped from Tim's face and spotted his shirt.

"You have nothing to be sorry for. You've done nothing wrong."

"But I lost my job, and now my family—"

"It's not your fault. You're a victim of the bad economy and circumstances beyond your control."

As we had for nearly thirty-one years, we sat across the table and held each other with our eyes. Seeing Tim's face lined with grief and exhaustion, I silently asked God to give us both strength and wisdom for our children's sake. "We can't talk about the past right now. We need to express hope for our future. Call Justin and Megan back to the table so we can talk. We need to get everyone calmed down," I said in a hushed voice.

As he'd done countless times over the years, Tim walked to the foot of the staircase and called to our children.

Please help Tim. Give him the right words for our kids, I prayed silently.

In minutes, all four of us were seated around the table again.

Tim took a deep breath. "We need to focus on the good things in our lives. God is providing money through your mother's inheritance, a place to store our belongings, apartments for both of you, and Aunt Emma's house for Mom and me. God is with us and He *will* get us through this."

"Dad," Megan interjected, "when will the four of us get together again?"

Tim looked at me before he replied. "I don't know when. I only know we will. With the four of us living in three different cities, we need to take things one day at a time."

After dinner, we gathered in the family room. Over the years, we had taken many photographs of our two children sitting on the fireplace hearth, but the ones we took of our sweet children that day are uniquely recognizable: their eyes are red from crying.

Late that afternoon, the four of us walked to our driveway where we hugged and kissed for the last time at our house. Before Justin and Megan got into their cars, we locked arms and stood in our family circle while Tim spoke. "No matter what happens, we need to remember that the Lord has a good plan for our future. God can't move us forward if we're looking behind."

Two weeks later, the movers arrived and filled the van with all of our possessions except the few things Tim and I needed to take with us. We knew people were praying for us because we felt God's strength and peace come over us as we watched the movers drive away.

Tim and I spent the next two days cleaning the empty house. We both wanted it to be spotless when the new owner took possession of it. When we walked out the door for the last time, the sun was low in the sky. I wept uncontrollably as I sat in the car waiting for Tim to lock up the house. His head was down as he walked to the car.

"Are we doing the right thing?" Tim's eyes searched mine as he held the house key in his hand.

"Yes." I pulled a tissue out of my handbag.

"But you and the kids are so upset. Maybe we shouldn't have sold the house."

"We're grieving. We *need* to grieve so we can move on. We all know this is the right thing to do."

"The right thing—not the easy thing." Tim looked up at the house, then started his SUV and backed out of the driveway.

We drove for several hours to get to my aunt's house. Although we'd stayed at Aunt Emma's house in the past, climbing into the guest-room bed that night felt surreal. I was grateful to be in a beautiful bedroom, but it didn't belong to us. Knowing my heart would ache all the more if I longed for our former house, I intentionally focused on thanking God for our temporary living quarters.

I climbed out of bed the next morning and looked out the window. I marveled at the blooming dogwood in the yard, every branch laden with deep pink flowers. The grass was emerald green and daffodils bloomed in the garden. I knew immediately that God provided this beautiful scene to soothe my jagged heart. He'd also given me the strength to leave my home. *I'm not a pillar of salt.* I smiled as I touched my warm cheek.

Our days at Aunt Emma's house stretched into months, and cold, snowy days announced the arrival of the holidays. Justin and Megan came to Aunt Emma's for Christmas. As we celebrated Christ's birth in a home that wasn't our own, it was tempting to long for our former life.

"Mom," Megan whispered, "there isn't a bedroom for Justin."

"Justin will have to use a blow-up mattress in the family room."

"But, Mom—"

"Megan, dearest, our lives have changed. We need to see the good in what we have and be grateful for it."

Our family encountered many challenges over the following months, but with God's help, we did our best to be grateful for the present while looking forward to the better times we prayed were ahead of us.

That October, Tim accepted a new job in another state. We bought a house that was only three hours away from each of our children. God was turning our lives around.

Ten days before Christmas, a moving company retrieved our possessions from storage and delivered them to our new house. While Tim worked at his new office, I unpacked boxes as fast as I could. Together, we anxiously awaited our children's arrival.

On Christmas Eve afternoon, jubilant voices reverberated through our new house when Justin and Megan arrived for the first time. It had been two years since we'd celebrated Christmas in a house of our own. Justin and Megan were anxious to walk through the rooms and were overjoyed when they looked upon their bedroom furniture and other possessions, sealed for so long in storage. That evening, we sat together around the same table that watched our little ones grow into young adults, ebullient joy signaling the end of our ordeal.

"I could never have imagined God's plan for us that Easter Sunday when everything looked so bad." Justin beamed as he looked around the room.

"God doesn't give us a preview of the future, Son," Tim responded, his voice content. "But he does tell us how to handle tough times."

"That's true," I agreed. "When I began packing up the old house, the story of Lot's wife came to me. We all know that two angels of the Lord told Lot to take his family and leave their home. It's the next part that most people miss: the angels intentionally instructed Lot's family to look forward because they knew it's not easy to walk away from the life you know."

"We could have been turned into pillars of salt," Megan noted with a smile, "but I never forgot what Dad told us in the driveway that last day at the house: God can only move us forward when we stop looking behind."

Name has been changed.

TIME TO REFLECT ON GOD'S PROVISION

I thought I *was* resting in God, but the true test came when my comfortable world fell apart.

Let the beloved of the Lord rest secure in Him,
for He shields him all day long,
and the one the Lord loves rests between his shoulders.

—Deuteronomy 33:12 (NIV)

14

WHEN HEALTH ISSUES AFFECT EMPLOYMENT OPTIONS

Carrie Fancett Pagels

See, I have refined you, though not as silver;
I have tested you in the furnace of affliction.

—Isaiah 48:10 (NIV)

While my husband and I lived in South Carolina—over twenty years ago—I had a terrible case of influenza. It was some kind of super flu that knocked half of the city's population on their backs, including my hubby, who was never ill. I experienced hot, searing pain in my joints that didn't disappear after my bout was over.

I'm a psychologist, and when I returned to work, I was shocked that I could barely walk from the pain in my feet. I also had trouble taking notes because of the pain in my hands and elbow. I was frightened—I'd never experienced anything like it and was terrified it might not go away. I didn't want to speak about it, because I was afraid that if I gave it a voice, the affliction would persist.

My family physician diagnosed me with osteoarthritis, because my rheumatoid blood tests were negative. A year later, my arthritis symptoms had calmed, and I thanked God. Then, the bottom dropped out.

The place where my husband worked as an engineer was closing. We were both shocked. Although I'd built up my private practice, I didn't believe I could support our little family on my income if we remained where we lived.

So, my husband interviewed with a company in New York. I was surprised when he accepted an offer, because he'd said he'd never move back to New York. It turned out that he meant he'd never move back to the New York City area. This new job was near Buffalo.

We were moving. After seeking legal advice on how to terminate my professional services, I sold what I could of my practice and referred all of my clients to other providers. My husband found a rental house in a rural area in eastern New York, and moved himself and our Labrador retriever ahead of our young daughter and me.

Meanwhile, in South Carolina, someone had been calling our house and hanging up. One night, someone tried to get in the house! The police came, and we found a crushed cigarette butt out back. We don't smoke. I was terrified. My daughter and I needed to be with Jeff in New York.

Later that year, both my daughter and I contracted mononucleosis and were very ill. My health took a huge nosedive.

The arthritis fatigue and pain returned with a roaring vengeance. I retired to bed each night at seven o'clock and didn't rise until twelve hours later. I was referred to a rheumatology practice and saw one of their youngest and newest doctors. He said my blood work didn't show Rheumatoid arthritis, although my symptoms did. He treated me for fibromyalgia and osteoarthritis with medications that had significant side effects.

A few months later, I sought licensure as a New York psychologist so I could resume working. Having graduated from an American Psychological Association-approved program—one of the top three school psychology doctoral programs in the United States—I was shocked to learn that a committee comprised of New York officials would have to go through my entire transcript to determine whether I would be eligible for a license. I had already been licensed and in practice in South Carolina for about five years. So, I sought out a school psychology certificate and was blessed to secure a part-time job that allowed me to be gone only a few days per week, while our daughter was in school.

My arthritis symptoms improved somewhat that spring and summer, but when winter hit, I was in agony. My husband and I prayed about it, and we agreed I would go to Atlanta, Georgia, to interview for a position with a prominent Christian treatment agency. I was offered a position. My husband and I then agreed we'd give it a try.

The temporary move was a disaster. Other than my arthritis symptoms improving dramatically in the more temperate climate, the rest of the trial period was a wash. I returned to New York

State after taking a psychology licensure exam in Georgia, hoping I could find another position in the South.

I received my Georgia licensure approval in an impossibly short time. A miracle, really, because I drove home to New York, and by the time I got there, my Georgia license approval was in the mailbox.

My symptoms returned while I was in New York. When I went back to the rheumatologist's office, I was seen by the senior doctor, a member of the New York medical licensing board. He took a look at my hot, red, painful elbow and rubbed his chin.

"You probably have Rheumatoid arthritis, but it doesn't show up in your blood. If you were staying here, I'd treat you for RA. I recommend that you find a rheumatologist in Georgia, once you move there, and see if they confirm your diagnosis."

Awhile later, a job became available to me in Georgia. I interviewed and was offered the position at a university, and we figured Jeff would look for a job once he joined us there. I notified the college that in order to accept their offer, I would also have to work in private practice in order for us to make the move, because the offered pay didn't cover our expenses.

The university agreed, so in addition to my job there, I joined a wonderful private practice. Several nights a week, I worked my second job as a private practice psychologist. The two psychologists who owned the practice were wonderfully supportive.

Little did I know, I was about to go through another valley experience. But God really does work things together for our good if we wait for Him, which also teaches patience. When we are in a valley and fully relying upon God, we begin to accept that life is not under our own power. When we trust in the Lord, faith grows—as does our relationship with Him.

Jeff was unable to find employment as a marine engineer in the small, landlocked city in Georgia. Being our sole breadwinner for years, this proved difficult for him. However, he was a wonderful stay-at-home dad. Without any engineering jobs, money got so tight that my husband applied to serve his additional Navy reservist duty. When he did so, the U.S. Navy refused him and also had him discharged from further reservist responsibilities. My nuclear shift test engineer-trained husband accepted a job at an automobile mechanic's shop so we could eat something better than the "gruel burgers" that I prepared from a bunch of weird ingredients. I remember being amazed by people who could afford to order pizza while our reduced finances forced us to develop our own inexpensive recipe for pizza that we ate at home.

Every month, we were financially short, but God convicted me to tithe. His blessings followed. When I looked for a rental house, God provided a Christian realtor who invited me to her church's Wednesday night supper. We enjoyed dining with them several Wednesday nights. Our church family was also an amazing refuge. My family and I remained on the prayer list at our home church for the entire time we faced our medical, financial, and work concerns. The fellowship was phenomenal, and we were very grateful for such a strong church home.

You've heard the expression "double for your trouble." We had such an experience with Jeff. For two years, we'd prayed so hard for him to get a job in Georgia. He finally did get a job, albeit as a contracted employee with a shipyard in Virginia. After beginning as an engineer again, he literally worked double the normal hours—sometimes as many as ninety hours in a week. My then-fourth-grade daughter and I stayed behind in Georgia. My husband lived out of a motel in Virginia for a few months as we awaited a full-time position with benefits to open up for at least one of us.

Things eventually settled down. My husband was picked up as a permanent employee by the shipyard. I accepted work as a public school psychologist. Our daughter entered an excellent Virginia school system. I found the best rheumatologist I have ever had. And—the Lord blessed us with another child, after thirteen years.

During every trial we faced, God was there. I am thankful for a husband willing to sacrifice his own employment for the sake of my health. Although my health deeply affected my husband's unemployment and served as a catalyst for the many trials we went through, God used every part of our story, providing a far better plan than we could have imagined.

TIME TO REFLECT ON GOD'S PROVISION

Broke?

No!

I am rich because I have God, my Great Provider
who supplies all of my needs.

I rejoice in following Your statutes as one rejoices in great riches.

—Psalm 119:14 (NIV)

15

TRUSTING FOR THE FUTURE
Ramona Richards

No one can receive anything unless it is given from Heaven.
—John 3:27 (CEB)

Jehovah-Jireh. God will provide. I had heard that name of God for years—in my Bible studies, and even on my job in Christian publishing. I had sung about it in choir; heard it preached from the pulpit. But I'd never prayed it; never been called on to believe in it without fail.

In April 2009, my carefully ordered world began to shift. In one way, I expected this. My daughter, who is severely disabled, would age out of the school system in May, so I needed to find alternative daily arrangements for her care. Easier said than done. Her nurse, Phyllis, took care of Rachel for part of the day, but she couldn't do it all day. Day programs for disabled adults are rare in our city. Those adults who are high functioning enough can find help in group homes or residential programs. Rachel, however, requires total care by a trained staff; she can do nothing for herself. But Rachel is active, personable, and loves socialization, so I didn't want her to sit at home all day, staring at the walls. Still, options were few.

I had not made a decision yet when my supervisor called me into his office. When I saw the Human Resources rep sitting beside him, I knew what was coming. My last day at work would be April seventeenth.

At first, the loss of my job seemed like a blessing. I could stay home with Rachel and freelance until I found a place for her and another job. I'd done this once before. I had a plan. I had not considered the economy, however, which began to fall away that year, or the changes that would come in publishing. The freelance work dried up quickly, and jobs grew scarce in Nashville. In addition, the freelance work I had done made me ineligible for unemployment.

The money became tight, then non-existent. My car payment was so far behind that I hid the car in the garage, fearing 2:00 a.m. repossession. The mortgage went unpaid. I tried to refinance, but the freelance jobs I could scrounge weren't enough security for the program to work. Foreclosure loomed, and I struggled even to pay for utilities and food with the child support that Rachel received.

While I searched for work, I pared back my lifestyle as much as I dared. I cut out the satellite service and the high speed Internet. I sold furniture, including the television. I had a sale and watched more than 400 of my beloved books leave with friends. Another 500 went to a used bookstore, netting enough to make a car payment.

I prayed, but no answer seemed forthcoming. Finally, I began to pray in a different way. Not for help. I prayed for my own sense of trust in God, in *Jehovah-Jireh.*

My church, hearing about my needs, took up a love offering that provided a needed infusion of cash into my bill paying efforts. Friends showed up with food staples to stretch the budget. Then, in May 2010, Phyllis put a radical plan on the table. Unbeknownst to me, she'd been deeply involved in her own prayer efforts about Rachel's situation.

Obviously, with few jobs available in Nashville, I needed to search for work elsewhere. So Phyllis proposed that Rachel move in with her. She'd take over care as her co-conservator, supported by her large family and circle of friends. This would take care of the placement issue for Rachel, and it would free me up to search wherever I needed to look. We met with Rachel's caseworker and began the process.

Almost simultaneously, I received an interview request for a job in New York City. Everything came together so quickly, I truly believed God was in this plan. The money was good ... no, it was *great!* More than I'd ever made. The first interview, conducted by phone, went well. The second, held at a restaurant in Nashville, went even better. A few days later, I received an email about flying to New York for the final interview.

I bounced around the house for days. This could save my financial future. I could get the mortgage caught up, maybe even rent the house while I was in New York. I had dreams of getting back on my feet faster than anyone expected.

Then, out of the blue, I received an email concerning a different job at a local company. Not only a job, but a *dream* job—the kind I'd wanted my entire career. Even though New York still sang in my mind, I filled out the application, feeling blessed. I received a call for an interview. A friend bought me a new outfit for the next two interviews; the local one came around first.

Unlike the initial interviews for the New York position, this one didn't go as well. I felt awkward and overdressed in my hose and heels. I thought I blew every question. I left thinking, "It'll never happen."

A few days later, I boarded the plane for New York for the final interview. I had a great time. Met everyone in the office. Received some great feedback. I left feeling elated and enthusiastic.

Then came that moment when all you can do is pray.

I had two job opportunities out there at the end of the rainbow, and I praised God. And I waited. When the call came, it was from the local company. Apparently, my interview had gone better than I thought. The dream job loomed. What stopped me cold, however, was the salary offer.

I felt desperate, grateful, and dismayed. My hopes of a new job blossomed while my aspirations for recovery shriveled. The offered money meant a serious pay cut from my previous career position, by more than a third. It would mean that I would not be able to catch up financially any time soon. It was the first time I received a job offer that left me in tears of despair.

At first, I thought, "There's still the other job, with the fabulous salary in a terrific new city." But New York went silent. When

I finally called for an update, the results left me with seriously mixed feelings. The good news was that I'd been chosen as one of two final candidates. The bad news was that the other candidate already lived in the city.

New York called to me, but the dream job was in the offering. Money argued with my heart. In a moment of deep prayer, however, I felt the reassurance: *Trust Me.*

I took the Abingdon Press job with prayers of thankfulness, but with a grim view of what came next. With a return to a full-time job but no day placement for Rachel, she would have to remain with Phyllis. This meant not only the salary cut but the loss of the child support. My income would be dropping by 40 percent. Serious changes were in store.

I would lose the house. Even if the mortgage had been current, I could no longer afford the payment. I rapidly readied the house and listed it on a short sale basis. The changes we had made for Rachel's wheelchair made it desirable, and a buyer appeared within a few weeks, even in a harsh, downturned market. He was a pre-qualified, disabled veteran, so the sale should have moved smoothly.

Six months later, however, the bank still stalled, with their foreclosure department sending me threatening letters even as their short sale division tried to work through the approval. My real estate agent had to talk me off the ledge of severe frustration and anger several times.

As that progressed, I moved from a three-bedroom house to a one-bedroom apartment that cost half as much—and had half the room. Much of my furniture had already been sold, and now

I gave away dishes and linens. Boxes of clothes and videos went to Goodwill or into the trash. More books and DVDs headed for the used bookstore.

My lifestyle changed significantly. Pleasure travel, even to see my mother, halted. Although I kept Rachel's hospital bed for some time, I had to accept that her move was permanent. My day no longer centered on her care needs, and the caregivers, who were also my friends, stopped coming to my home every day. Neighbors I casually chatted with on a daily basis disappeared from my life.

Even with the financial cutbacks, every penny had to be considered and budgeted. I adjusted to apartment life, suddenly having neighbors above and beside me, and taking my clothes to the Laundromat again. Any extra money had to be saved for tires, oil changes, and emergencies. Restaurants and movies became treats from friends. I soon discovered how much free entertainment could be had around Nashville.

Then there was the job. It was, in fact, my dream job, my "sweet spot." I loved every minute of it, every day, even when frustrations, problems, and changes occurred. I adored my colleagues and my supervisor, and I continue to enjoy all the authors I get to work with. Despite the financial shift, it was the right choice.

I also began to see that *Jehovah-Jireh* isn't just a name for God in the present. It's also how He works in the past and in the future.

You see, I believe God had prepared me for this time with all that had come before. A few years ago, He put on my heart to rid myself of as much debt as possible, so I had no credit card payments, just the house and the car. I've had a nomadic spirit all my life. I've never lived in one place for more than a few years, which lessened the wrench of losing the house.

I've never really had any emotional attachment to many of my possessions, and anytime I do, something happens to remind me of the impermanence of this world. A computer crash in 1995 destroyed more than 300 short stories and a novel, which will never be recovered. My wedding dress was stolen, as was my grandmother's antique trunk. In one of my previous relocations, the movers crushed a woodworking piece my father made.

Then, of course, there's Rachel, who reminds me that even our dreams for our children are mere illusions that can be shattered at any moment.

This time, I truly believe God put a reminder on my heart that reliance on money, a particular job, or any imagined future is foolish—and that He had given me the ability to deal with the shock of change. He wanted me to trust Him—not just for the here and now but for my future as well.

Because He wasn't finished.

As I settled into the new lifestyle and routine at home, shifts continued at work. Before long, I had a new supervisor—a wise, experienced woman who has become a true mentor. And shortly after that ... a promotion and a raise.

I haven't returned to those pre-unemployment days financially, but I've paid off my car and moved into a duplex with more room. I own no home, but I have no debt either. The budget is still tight, but I have a meager savings account for emergencies. I have health care again.

I also have a renewed sense of and reliance on *Jehovah-Jireh*. While everything in this world—friends, family, possessions, jobs, money—are fleeting and temporary, the one thing that never changes is God and His love and provision for us.

TIME TO REFLECT ON GOD'S PROVISION

"We owe *how* much in taxes?
You've *got* to be kidding!"

*Lord, thank You for Your holy word that
tells me to be anxious for nothing.*

16

THE ALPHA AND OMEGA PROVIDES

La-Tan Roland Murphy

"I am the Alpha and the Omega," says the Lord God,
"Who is, and Who was, and Who is to come, the Almighty."
—Revelation 1:8 (NIV)

New Year's Day ushers in a feeling of excitement and when I think of it, I reflect on past holiday experiences. Warm memories flood my heart as I recall many years of watching Dick Clark as he commentated each New Year's Eve event in Times Square. In my mind, I hear him shouting, "Happy New Year, everyone!" after the historic ball dropped. Shouts and cheers from the crowd filled the night air. A new year had begun.

My sweetest memories of years gone by are of New Year's Eve parties, complete with explosive fireworks, good food, and time spent with family and friends. With *the old* out and *the new* in, like most Americans, I feel a sense of encouragement in knowing a brand new year holds potential for fresh starts and new beginnings. With pen in hand, I eagerly make my hope-filled list of resolutions. I promise to lose weight, start an exercise program, and strive to live my life more intentionally. Unseen fireworks explode in my heart as I embrace the sense of newness I feel inside. With fresh calendar pages before me, I eagerly look forward with expectancy to new adventures from the beginning of January to the end of December.

New Year's Day 2008 proved to be a sad start to a brand new calendar year. I was sleepy from our late night family fun and I longed to sleep in. The blankets beckoned me to stay snuggled in my warm, comfy cocoon, but the phone was intent on ringing-in my new year. With squinted eyes, I struggled to reach the phone. "Hello," I whispered in a soft, groggy voice. I was not prepared for my year to begin this way.

"He's gone." My older brother's voice quivered with emotion. Although I had been expecting the call, never in my wildest dreams had I imagined it would come on New Year's Day—not that a phone call like this would have been easier to swallow on any other day of the year.

The news of my brother's passing left me in a state of disbelief. Somewhere in the quiet recesses of my hopeful heart, I thought he would be healed. He was, after all, invincible—at least to me. He was strong, athletic, and an amazing godly leader.

Surely the Lord needed him to stay here with us. Surely He needed his godly influence in the lives of others. My thoughts exploded like fireworks as the force of this news burst in the invisible dark cloud hanging above my bed—a very different kind of New Year's fireworks than I could have ever imagined.

I swallowed hard while trying to catch my breath. "He's gone," I said to my husband as I rolled over, planting my tearstained face into his chest. It was a loud, heartbroken cry. It was like an out-of-body experience. I could hear a deep, painful cry that came from way down inside of me. Every part of my being felt grief stricken. My husband held me patiently until I could no longer produce tears.

Just a week before, I had anxiously sat in the waiting room of the cancer center, holding a box filled with empty vials on my lap. Joy filled my heart because the box represented hope for my brother's survival. I was there to be tested for a bone marrow match. The nurse called me back to the small room where they would draw my blood to send back to my brother's hospital in Atlanta, Georgia. I was so excited—convinced I would be a match.

My cell phone rang. It was my sister-in-law, telling me my brother's health had taken a turn for the worse. The doctors didn't think he would make it through the night. There was no need to have the test done. It was too late.

I walked slowly back to my car. The sunlight was bright and beautiful. I sat frozen in place, staring out across the parking lot, the same small box lying in my lap. With tears streaming down my face, I cried out to God, telling him how sad I was that it had been too late and how I was sure I would have been a perfect match for my brother. *I* was telling the great *I AM* that my brother might have lived if *I* had been able to get tested earlier.

Now, days later, he was gone, and a deep, dark depression settled over my spirit that would remain for days and weeks to come. I felt like someone had wrapped my entire being in black blankets. I went through each day in a numbed-down, robotic motion. Not only was I in emotional despair, my husband and I were also in financial despair.

I was forced to take a corporate job in order to keep my family afloat. Our credit card debt was mounting because my husband's company could not afford to pay him a salary. In the midnight hour, God provided a job for me. I enjoyed training the new-hire teachers and the interaction with the directors and parents, but it was difficult to work at maximum capacity while my world fell apart around me. Being the main provider left me feeling as if the weight of the world were on my shoulders. Though I was honored to be a helpmate in providing for our family, I still struggled with the loss of my brother. The burden of my brother's death, along with our impending financial despair, felt too much to bear.

To make things worse, three months after my brother passed, I came home from work and found my husband waiting for me. I could tell by the look on his face that something terrible had happened. He gently broke the news. His business partner had stopped monthly payments toward our health insurance policy. As a result of his irresponsibility, we had unknowingly been without insurance coverage for over a month.

Grief and exhaustion, coupled with anger, overcame me. I collapsed onto the floor and cried out to God. *How could this be happening? My security has been pulled out from under me. I'm so angry, Lord. I thought this year would bring blessings. What if one of us had been seriously ill or had been diagnosed with cancer during this breach of insurance coverage—what would we have done, Lord? How selfish of this man to do this and not even tell us we had no insurance coverage. Anything could have happened during this time, Lord.*

I found myself blurting out one panic-stricken prayer after another, telling the Alpha and Omega where my security lay. I was angry because I had high hopes this New Year would bring financial success. Financial despair had worn my emotions down. I was amazed at how affected I was by these circumstances and disappointed in my faithless behavior.

My husband and I were stunned by a blast of news we received from the insurance company. They informed us that I would have to pay $1,600 per month in order to have health insurance. I was "medically un-coverable" from the insurance company's perspective. To make things worse, we were unable to reach a live person at the insurance company—only a recording that gave us the runaround. We wanted answers. After many phone calls, we were finally told my medical records read: Von Willebrand Disease, a *rare blood disorder*. Because of this, I had been labeled "high risk." We continued attempting to speak with a person, to no avail.

During this time, my husband's faith grew stronger while mine fell apart. Looking back, I realize that even in this, God provided newfound strength to persevere. This was a gift—that my husband could be strong—for I needed someone to lean on. I was disappointed in the way I had responded to the devastations this year had brought with it, knowing in my head and heart that God would provide as He always had. But my emotions were busy setting off explosive fireworks—especially with the news from the insurance company—keeping me in a constant state of nervousness and alarm.

I felt a sense of deep guilt that my faith had proven itself weak. I had prided myself in faithfully trusting the God of my childhood to provide for me. I had not grown up with financial abundance, but had been privileged to witness God's great provisions manifested time and time again during tough seasons. I had come to rest in the Alpha and Omega who had been there from the beginning. I knew in my heart He would not fail us now, but my flesh kept crying out from the weight of what seemed like over-bearing, external circumstances.

My husband and I enrolled in a financial management class in order to get an over-all financial game plan. While there are many "get out of debt" financial programs offered today, we found one that was biblically based, had a common sense approach, and lined up with the desire of our hearts to be good investors as well as givers.

God went ahead of us, getting His insurance plan ready, even before we signed up for the class. Through a series of events, we were introduced to a reputable insurance broker. Our hearts were encouraged to think we could possibly be provided affordable health insurance coverage. My husband called the broker nearest us and explained all that had happened to us. The insurance broker instructed me to collect five years of medical records from every doctor I had seen, promising to personally settle the matter. The process took more than two years to clear up.

On Christmas Eve, the phone rang. Unlike my earth-shattering New Year's call, this was a welcomed call from the insurance broker.

"I'm sorry for calling on Christmas Eve, but my son is flying into RDU Airport tonight. I know you guys live near the airport, and I thought I'd drop by to pick up your medical records. I plan to be at your insurance company's office bright and early the day after Christmas in order to get this cleared up."

We felt so blessed by the thought that this man would give up his precious family time on Christmas Eve in order to drive to our home for my medical records. As promised, the day after Christmas, our amazing insurance broker went to our insurance company, met with someone face-to-face, and explained how they had made a mistake on my records.

We discovered the mistake had been made in my records years before when I had a tumor removed from my back. Although the tumor had been non-cancerous, I had developed a very large blood clot and had to have it surgically removed. The doctors had been puzzled as to why a blood clot formed and they sent me to the cancer centers to be tested for Von Willebrand's Disease. Though the test was negative, the insurance assessor had looked incorrectly at the written form and thought I was *positive* for this rare blood disorder. Hence, I was considered high risk and had been refused coverage.

Without realizing it, I became paralyzed by fear. I had unknowingly elevated an insurance policy above God's ability to provide for me in sickness and in health. I humbly asked my heavenly Father, who tells me in His word He knows the number of hairs on my head, to forgive me and help me in my unbelief. He tenderly reminded me that He would not leave me to suffer alone. He promised to be with me from the start of my days to their end. He is the first and the last, the beginning and the end. He is Almighty God. My insurance policy was written by Him in blood when He willingly gave Himself up on the cross for my sins. It was on the cross He lovingly looked out through time and saw each need I would have throughout my entire life. He knew I would be tempted to put my security in external, man-made things like insurance policies.

God provided for us in very specific ways. Fear had whispered into my ear way too long, telling me I would get sick like my brother and not have proper health insurance. My Savior rescued me, gently freeing me from the enemy's grip.

Our faith grew through this painful time in our lives. We now realize God was there on January first, and throughout the year, providing for us in amazing ways and setting my records straight. He *is* our insurance and our security. He is the beginning and the end of all things, including our calendar days. He is our great provider. His power is more explosive than any event our days will bring. No matter the trials of life, God has a plan for provision in tough times for those who believe.

Expect good days ahead. Even on our worst days, He is working for our good.

Happy New Year, everybody!

TIME TO REFLECT ON GOD'S PROVISION

The demands of life are often so overwhelming.
How could I make it in my own strength?

For the eyes of the Lord range throughout the earth
to strengthen those whose hearts are fully committed to Him.
—2 Chronicles 16:9 (NIV)

17

LOSING A JOB IS PERSONAL
Tamara D. Fickas

But now, this is what the Lord *says—*
He who created you, Jacob, He who formed you, Israel:
"Do not fear, for I have redeemed you;
I have summoned you by name; you are mine.
When you pass through the waters, I will be with you;
and when you pass through the rivers,
they will not sweep over you.
When you walk through the fire, you will not be burned;
the flames will not set you ablaze.

—Isaiah 43:1-2 (NIV)

In January 2007, my world changed when the CEO of the company I worked for called an important meeting. As a coworker and I traveled to the corporate office, she wondered what was going on, but I wasn't worried. However, I quickly found that the CEO's message wasn't good. The financial outlook was bleak, and lay-offs were the only option. Those affected would meet with their directors that day.

That afternoon, my boss confirmed my job had been eliminated.

Being unemployed was new to me, and I had no idea that the emotional aspects of unemployment would be just as overwhelming as the financial. In the months that followed, I would learn that regardless of why a person ends up unemployed, it can deal a devastating blow to their self-esteem and bring on varying emotions. Losing a job is personal and cuts to the core of our being.

In February, just a week after my health insurance ran out, I had what I thought was a cold. It lingered, and I developed an excruciating headache. I finally gave in and went to my doctor, who sent me to the emergency room for a spinal tap. Within hours, I was diagnosed with meningitis and sepsis and was admitted to the hospital.

As I lay in the hospital bed with an IV pumping fluids and antibiotics into my body, I wondered how I was going to pay the mounting bill. One afternoon I received a call from the Human Resources department at the company I had worked for. The employee heard I was in the hospital, and she wanted me to know I still had time to sign up for COBRA, the insurance continuation coverage required by law. Without a job and on limited income, the question was: could I find a way to pay the premiums? My fear of losing my house to pay off hospital bills was somewhat abated, but the pressure of needing to find a job intensified.

One thing I'd never had trouble with was finding a job. Anytime I wanted to make a move, I was able to go out and find a new employer. That all changed with my lay-off. Under the terms of my state unemployment compensation, I was required to submit a minimum number of applications each week. Each day, I checked the want ads in the paper and online job sites. I pursued any jobs I was qualified for and followed all leads from friends and former coworkers. I tried to think outside of the box for other ways my experience could work in different fields. The months wore on, and it became harder to find positions that were a match for my education and experience.

It was disheartening to send out so many applications and not receive a call or email in response. I could rationalize that some of the jobs I applied for weren't a good fit. It stung my pride, though, when I didn't get calls on positions I knew I was qualified—or even over-qualified—to do. Worse still were jobs I interviewed for, but didn't get hired. There were two particular situations that dealt big blows to my ego.

In the first situation, I met with the hiring manager. She hinted at a second interview. Later that day, I sent off a thank you email. I waited. Nothing happened. Days turned into a week without a call. After an appropriate time, I made a follow-up call and left a message. I never did hear back from the manager, so I never knew what happened.

A month or so later, I sent an application to another company in response to an advertisement. After my initial interview, I felt good about the possibility. I learned that one of the hiring managers and I had a mutual friend who was more than willing to give me a recommendation. When called for a second round of interviews, I believed even more that I had a good chance at the job.

A day after the second interview, I received the call. It was a close race between me and another applicant. That person had the certification needed for the position; I did not. I was more than willing to pursue the certification, but they chose the other person.

At that point, I felt beaten down. My thoughts turned to whether or not I would ever work again. I couldn't fathom that. I knew I had to have some way to support myself, but after months of hunting for a job, it seemed I might not find one.

For the first time in my unemployment journey, I felt like a loser. I replayed the interviews in hopes of figuring out what went wrong. When I couldn't pinpoint any one thing, I cried out to God. I couldn't believe He dangled carrots in front of my nose and then yanked them away. I couldn't see His plan and that frustrated me.

Regardless of appearances, I couldn't help think that maybe this whole time was a blessing in disguise. My mom was several years into a battle with Lewy Body Dementia. This form of dementia had slowly stolen her ability to do much for herself. Dad did an amazing job as her primary caregiver, but it wasn't a one-person job. I recognized this time without work obligations was God's way of allowing me to help them. This gave me comfort in the midst of swirling emotions.

In our culture, a common conversation starter begins, "What do you do for a living?" Much of how we define ourselves is often tied up in our title and the things we do during our working hours. This was me. I had been proud of my work, and without a job, I didn't know how to answer the question of what I did.

I looked for other ways to define who I was. For the first few months, I told people I was on sabbatical or hiatus. Later, I found new purpose in my life, and that purpose didn't have anything to do with my job.

In June of 2007, Dad was diagnosed with blockage in his cardiac arteries and scheduled for urgent open-heart surgery. During the significant recovery time, he wouldn't be able to care for Mom. I moved into their house a few days before his surgery and didn't move back to my own home for four months. It dawned on me that if I'd gotten either one of the jobs I had wanted so desperately, this time would have been much harder for Mom and Dad, since I wouldn't have been there when they needed me.

The months after Dad's surgery were filled with laundry, housecleaning, cooking, and taking care of my mom. I'd always dreamed of getting married and caring for my husband and family. Here, in the midst of everything, God fulfilled the underlying desires behind my dream—nurturing a family. I had found new purpose in my life. When people asked what I did for a living, I told them I was a stay-at-home daughter. Although I'm not pleased that my parents had to go through such a hard time, I am thrilled that God called me by name to be there, with them, through it all.

By the fall of 2007, my unemployment payments ran down to the wire, and I had no idea how I would continue to pay all the bills after they ran out. Fear niggled its way around the edges of my life. I tried to keep it at bay. I still lived with my parents, and I didn't want them to know my concern.

In those moments of fear, I acknowledged another emotion—
anger. Thoughts about why my job was eliminated played out in
my brain. Ultimately, the loss of a big contract was the main
reason behind the company's decision. Still, I tried to second-
guess the choices that were made, despite not being privy to all
the information. Anger was an unexpected emotion during my
unemployment, but another one took me completely by surprise.

Over the years, my mother often told me that a person is only
as old as they feel. I've always felt pretty young, but as time wore
on without a new job, I wondered if my age had anything to do
with not being hired. Granted, I was only in my early forties and
have never looked my age. However, as part of my separation
interview with the Human Resources Director, he gave me a list
of all the positions affected by the lay-off and the ages of the
employees in those jobs. This was proof that I wasn't being laid
off because of my age. At the time, I laughed it off. Because, as I
said, I didn't feel old. After months of "pounding the pavement"
and not finding the right job, even thoughts of being too old
filled my mind.

I spent ten months unemployed. I eventually returned to
work, just as my unemployment benefits ran out. The roller
coaster of highs and lows I rode during those months was often
scary and depressing, but God was there through it all. It is often
said that in times of crisis in our lives, our faith grows the most,
and it was certainly true for me that year. As in Isaiah 43:1, I
walked through the water, and it hadn't swept over me; I had
walked through fire and not been burned.

God has called me by name, and even without a job I am His. My mom passed away in October of 2007, just as I returned to work. I am so thankful for the time I had with her because of the lay-off. The memories of special moments with her during that time are tucked away in my heart. As I look back on those days, I can honestly say that even in the darkness, God was with me and had a plan for me.

TIME TO REFLECT ON GOD'S PROVISION

When my friends betray me,
You are ever faithful, ever true.

*You will be betrayed even by parents, brothers,
relatives, and friends.*

—Luke 21:16 (NIV 1984)

18

WHERE DOES MY SECURITY LIE ... REALLY?

Dan Walsh

For you shall not go out in haste, and you shall not go in flight,
for the Lord *will go before you, and the God of Israel*
will be your rear guard.

—Isaiah 52:12 (ESV)

At the end of the summer of 2010, after serving as a pastor in the same church for twenty-five years, I suddenly found myself unemployed. What happened? Something my wife and I would never have imagined. I was forced into pastoral "retirement" by a handful of influential people in our church I had once considered friends.

I wasn't found guilty of immorality or any financial misdeeds. My family life was in good shape. My pink slip was the result of church politics. I could explain the details, but, honestly, it's a miserable story. The bottom line was I could either leave quietly with a meager severance pay or stay and fight. To do so would have likely caused a church split and, because of the tightness in the church's finances, I knew it would have gone belly up. My wife and I hadn't labored the last twenty-five years only to destroy the church on our way out.

So, there we were, in terrible emotional pain with three months of income, no church, no job, and no provision when that money ran out. We didn't even have unemployment compensation to draw from. I had seen this trouble coming for a few months, so we had cashed out most of my pension to pay off the remaining balance on our house—which we had lived in for all of those twenty-five years. But without a job, I couldn't even afford the taxes and insurance, let alone the water, telephone, and light bill.

My health had deteriorated terribly in the months leading up to this time. Actually, my doctor had informed me that if I didn't find a way to reduce my stress, I was in danger of a heart attack or stroke. My wife and I both knew the source of the stress; it was the pain and heartache we were experiencing.

Oddly enough, even with all the uncertainty we suddenly faced, my health began to dramatically improve the week after I left. I learned there are worse things than being unemployed.

Something else I learned was that my trust, apparently for many years, wasn't fully in the Lord but on the church and the steady paycheck it had provided for so many years. Suddenly, I was faced with the worries and anxieties many in my congregation had dealt with over the past few years, due to the economic recession.

And I didn't like it. Not one bit.

There was nothing I could do. I'd made a decision—with my wife's full support—that would keep the church from financial ruin. But, unless God came through for us in a big way, our own situation was in serious jeopardy.

In the years leading up to this dilemma, I experienced a personal revival. I had been walking with the Lord all along (That's nice to hear, isn't it, considering I was a pastor?), but I had become more of a Martha than a Mary. In 2006, all that changed. God brought me through some personal difficulties that helped me see the extent of this drift, and I repented wholeheartedly. From then on, I made my devotional life a serious priority.

This daily pursuit of God continued—even increased—in the months preceding this ordeal. In one of those quiet times, the verse in Isaiah 52 (the one I cited at the beginning) popped out at me. As I read, it was as if the Lord spoke it to me personally. I even wrote it in my journal that way.

By then, my first two novels, *The Unfinished Gift* and *The Homecoming*, had already released (writing fiction had become my spare-time hobby). My twenty-fifth anniversary as a pastor was just around the corner. For several years, my wife and I had discussed with some of the key leaders in the church that this might be the right time for me to "pass the baton" while I began to take a lesser role in the church. I considered serving as a staff pastor and administrator. Then, maybe in a few years, if book sales allowed, I might even be able to go part-time and write part-time.

There was no way I could possibly see us making it through on my writing alone. Everything I'd read said this was an impossible goal. Over 95 percent of published writers have a "day job," because they don't earn enough to make it on writing alone. The money I'd made so far seemed to confirm this. And although I was genuinely weary of leading the church after all those years, I still enjoyed much of the work of pastoral ministry and felt God still wanted me to stay.

So, when I read this verse in Isaiah 52, I didn't interpret it to mean I would be abruptly leaving the church in a couple of months. More like a couple of years, if I left the church at all (except perhaps to retire, in my sixties). It turned out, I had interpreted things incorrectly. That's putting it mildly; I was way off. I now believe the Lord was trying to prepare me for something He saw coming up ahead. Something I would never have imagined or ever allowed myself even to consider, let alone prepare for.

Thankfully, we serve a sovereign God who knows the future and everything that's going to happen in all of the days written in our book (Psalm 139:16). He had gone ahead of us and prepared for us a river in the desert and a roadway in the wilderness. At the time, though, I didn't see it. Not even with eyes of faith. I felt like the apostles must have felt the day after Christ's crucifixion.

My world had suddenly been torn apart and turned upside down. I was in my mid-50s, had been a pastor for twenty-five years, earned a pretty good salary and full benefits, and now everything in my future was completely uncertain. The passage in Isaiah 52, right then, felt like a lie. At least the first part: *For you shall not go out in haste, and you shall not go in flight …* My departure from the church and my sudden unemployment felt very "hasty" and sudden to me.

Shortly after this, I came across that passage again. I asked the Lord to explain. I wasn't shaking my fist at heaven, charging God with injustice; I was just confused. Why would He have stirred my heart months ago when I read this passage, when He knew full well the horrible thing we were going to experience now? As I quietly waited in His presence, I experienced the peace of God wash over me and calm my fears. Then, it was as if the Holy Spirit began taking me through something of a review of the past few years of my life. I could see a number of examples where the Lord tried to get through to me and prepare me for the very thing we experienced.

But, I was unwilling, because of fear, to even consider it. I couldn't imagine how God could provide for us apart from the church, so I was unwilling to consider that He may have to. Because of this, I couldn't see (or wouldn't see) all the danger signs that trouble brewed. Sadly, my wife did. Even my secretary did. Both tried to warn me, but I couldn't see or grasp what they were saying.

There's a reason. It's hard to pick up something new when your hands are completely full. My hands were completely full, holding onto life—and everything in life as I had known it for years—as tightly as I could. I didn't realize my heart had shifted, and my security was no longer in God alone but in the earthly provision He had used all those years. And because it was, when the end came, I didn't see it coming, and it felt like we were leaving "in haste."

But, very soon, the second half of Isaiah 52:12 came into play. Almost immediately, God opened doors of provision I had never considered or could have opened on my own.

My wife was hired at the first job she applied for, as an office manager for a new Hobby Lobby opening in our town. Things began to happen with my books. The first one actually won two ACFW Carol Awards. Both were getting excellent reviews from magazines, bloggers, and fans. This resulted in my publisher offering me a three-book contract for the next eighteen months, writing two books a year. And, my agent was able to secure a second book contract with Guideposts for a new series they had just begun.

Barely a month after this, I got another call from my publisher with some astounding news. Bestselling author and relationship expert, Dr. Gary Smalley, had been searching for a new fiction author to work with on a new series of novels, similar to the best-selling series he had written with co-author Karen Kingsbury a few years back. In his search, he had come across my first two novels and absolutely loved them. He told me later that as soon as he finished the books, he knew his search was over; I was the one he wanted to work with on the new series.

This resulted in another four-book contract. Suddenly, I had enough work for the next three years doing something I loved to do and making enough money to live on. We weren't wealthy by any means, but it was enough that my wife didn't have to keep working at Hobby Lobby. I knew there was something else Cindi had wanted to do for as long as I've known her (we've been married thirty-six years).

She loves dogs. We both do. She wanted to be a certified dog trainer, but that dream got set aside when I became a pastor and she became a pastor's wife. After I left the church, the job at

Hobby Lobby wasn't something she wanted to do but something we needed her to do to help pay the bills. Now I could turn her loose to pursue her dream.

She spent most of 2011 going through Animal Behavior College, graduating with a 4.0 GPA. To become certified, she needed to intern at our local Humane Society. A few months after she graduated, they offered her a job. Not just any job. They created a new position for her. She is now their Animal Behavior Manager, and she's getting to do something she's always wanted to do—train dogs. And she's getting paid to do it.

Financially, we're still not where we were when I retired from pastoral ministry. My pension is still a wreck. We have medical insurance at a much-reduced level. Our household budget is much leaner and meaner. But, we're very happy. God has faithfully provided all we need and then some. Seeing all of the doors that opened, it's clear that God certainly did go before us and prepare the way. That feeling of being abandoned was just that, a feeling.

God remained faithful to His Word and faithful to us. And, just like the Word says, He uses our trials and circumstances to refine us and teach us His ways. I would never have volunteered to go through this ordeal, but I can honestly say God has used it to reveal that my trust was no longer in Him but in the earthly means he had chosen for a time. A long time, but just for a time.

Now, I look to Him and only to Him, as I should have all along. And, I don't have to worry about what's coming next, because God hasn't just gone before us, He has also become "our rear guard."

TIME TO REFLECT ON GOD'S PROVISIONS

What do you mean when you say, "Envision your dreams?"
We've been through so much, I'm fresh out of dreams!

*Now faith is being sure of what we hope for
and certain of what we do not see.*

—Hebrews 11:1 (NIV 1984)

19

ENVISION YOUR BLESSING
Cynthia Howerter

Jesus looked at them and said,
"With man this is impossible,
But with God all things are possible."
—Matthew 19:26 (NIV)

Every spring, the rhododendrons in our garden treated us to an abundance of lavender blossoms and rich green leaves. A friend asked what made our shrubs thrive. "The only way to promote growth is to provide nourishment and get rid of everything that's dead. I fertilize regularly, remove the spent blossoms, and cut out the dead branches," I explained. Just like a gardener, God continually strengthens our faith by feeding it with His knowledge and systematically pruning out the weak parts. During the twenty-one months of my husband's unemployment, God used some people to strengthen my faith by teaching me His wisdom, while He used others to remove the weak parts that impeded its growth.

After my husband's job loss, we sold our house and moved halfway across Pennsylvania to stay with my Aunt Emma* while Tim searched for a job. Soon after settling in, my friend Reverend Kate,* a Presbyterian minister, called to check on us. After hearing that Tim had no new job leads and that I was discouraged, Kate told me to get a notebook and write down everything I would like to have in our next house.

At first, I thought Kate was joking. I didn't see the point in doing this, because Tim didn't have a job. "Besides, even if Tim finds another job, if he doesn't earn enough, we won't be able to buy another house."

"You'll get another house." Kate's voice was authoritative.

"Kate, are you listening to me? Tim doesn't even have an interview lined up. He can't get a job if no one interviews him."

She continued, "Do you want a garage?"

"Kate—"

"You probably want a two-car garage. Do you want it dry-walled? If it's dry-walled, it should be painted."

"Kate, are you—"

"Write it down. Write down everything you want in your next house."

"We need Tim to get a job first. If Tim doesn't get a job soon, we'll never be able to buy another house. We're going to be running out of money by—"

"How many bathrooms do you want?"

"I can't see us ever buying another house. I think we may be done financially."

"That's what faith is all about, precious one. Faith is believing God for what you cannot see. I want you to envision the blessing that God is going to give you. Make a detailed list of everything you want in your next house and pray about it. Keep the list so that when you move into your next house, you can pull it out and show people how God answered your prayers."

"I don't know, Kate. It doesn't seem possible."

"What else are you doing right now?"

"I should be writ—"

"You also need to make a wish list for Tim's next job."

"What?"

"Yeah, but use a separate paper for that. And be thorough. Write down everything you'd like Tim to have in his next job."

I rolled my eyes. Sometimes people just didn't get it. My husband hadn't worked in six months, there were no job interviews on the horizon, we didn't qualify for unemployment, the severance pay had stopped, and our savings were dwindling as we struggled to pay our bills on time so we could avoid a bad credit rating.

Kate was on a roll and wouldn't stop. "Let's see, what about salary? Figure out how much you want Tim to earn and write it down. He probably should have a 401-K plan, don't you think?"

"Kate, this is crazy. It's like picking out a wedding dress when you don't even have a boyfriend." Did she even hear what I said?

"Benefits."

No, she must not have.

"Hmm, you'll need dental and health care. Anything else?"

"A prescription plan." I held my forehead in my hand as a sudden headache approached.

"See? You're getting the picture. Revise both lists until you're happy with them."

"But—"

"Do it."

"All right."

"What?"

"I will, I will."

It's impossible to say no to Reverend Kate.

Kate was right about one thing: other than writing, I had little else to do. So, I found a notebook and wrote detailed wish lists for our next house and Tim's next job. Over the next two weeks, I revised the lists multiple times until I was satisfied with them, and then—because Kate told me to—I prayed over both. I realized that I really did want everything on my lists. I wanted them badly. I kept the notebook next to my computer, and whenever I glanced at it, I prayed.

Tim and I had many Christian friends who stayed in touch with us during our time at Aunt Emma's. Initially, every one of them tried to encourage us whenever they phoned. As Tim's unemployment continued, some advised us to accept that God was closing the door on Tim getting a job—especially one that paid well. I felt hurt and betrayed to be told by a person of faith that God didn't have a good plan for Tim. That contradicted the scripture from Jeremiah 29:11: *"For I know the plans I have for you,"* declares the Lord, *"plans to prosper you and not to harm you, plans to give you hope and a future."*

Not long after these conversations, Kate called and wanted to know how Tim and I were doing. "It's been eight months. Tim's had one interview. Several weeks afterward, the company instituted a hiring freeze. He searches every day, but the economy's so terrible that hardly any companies are hiring. Do you think God's going to give Tim a job, or should we just give up hope?"

"God has a reason for allowing you and Tim to go through this. Right now, you, Tim, and I don't understand the why of it, but we can absolutely expect God to get you through this."

"I can't take much more."

"You said that three months ago, and you're still managing."

"All right, then, let me put it this way: I don't *want* to go through any more of this."

"That's a different story. This will end when God says it'll end. Not one second sooner. Not one second later. In the meantime, He's getting you through this, whether you like it or not."

I wiped my tears with the back of my hand.

"Oh. Don't sit there and hope God gets you and Tim through this. Expect it."

"Why should we expect it?"

"Because the Bible—God's own words—says, *'The Lord will work out His plans for my life—for your loving kindness, Lord, continues forever'* (Psalm 138:8). It's also written, *'The righteous cry, and the Lord hears and delivers them out of all their troubles'* (Psalm 34:17). We can both trust and expect God to do what He says He'll do."

Because Kate explained why Tim and I should expect God to answer our prayers for employment, I did. I believed God could give Tim a job—and not just any job, but a good-paying job. As soon as someone told me that Tim would never get another job, I focused on God's promises and two of my favorite Bible stories, Daniel and David.

Several months later, I had an appointment with Dr. Jane,* a local doctor whom I had seen the year before. After telling her that my husband had now been unemployed for fifteen months, she chewed me out. "When are you and your husband going to face reality? He's never going to get another good-paying job. The two of you are living in a fantasy world to think otherwise. You need to accept that the best job your husband can hope for is a janitorial position. The days of him earning a self-supporting salary are gone. You're facing public housing and public assistance."

I was so shocked that I could barely speak, but somehow I managed to look Dr. Jane in the eye and say, "You have no idea how powerful my God is, or you would not be saying such things to me."

She curled her lips. "God can't get you out of your predicament."

"I believe He can." I surprised myself as I spoke with authority.

At the end of my appointment, I hurried to my car and sat behind the steering wheel, tears dripping onto my blouse. I didn't want to go back to Aunt Emma's house and have Tim see me upset, because I knew he'd want to know what happened. Instead, I called a close friend who encouraged me to focus on the Old Testament story, "The Twelve Spies" (Numbers 13-14).

After carefully reading this story, I understood that my faith in God boils down to one word: believe. Do I believe that God can do what He says He can—or do I not believe it?

Dr. Jane's verbal thrashing required me to further prune my faith. Would I choose to be like Caleb and Joshua and believe that God had the type of job on my wish list in store for Tim, or would I choose to doubt His power like the other ten spies and miss out on God's blessing for us? I knew my answer.

Shortly after this, I spent time with our daughter Megan. I could see that she was troubled, so I asked her to tell me what was upsetting her. She burst into tears, crying so hard she could barely speak. "Mom, I'm so afraid Dad's never going to get another job and that you'll be poor the rest of your lives."

Without hesitation, a powerful voice that was not mine spoke through my mouth. "The story's not over yet!" I was as shocked by the words as my daughter was. God used those words spoken by His Holy Spirit to strengthen our faith. I told Megan the story of the twelve spies and explained that, not only did we have to believe that God would give Tim a good job, we needed to expect that He would.

The months of fertilizing and pruning my faith and my family's faith were fraught with droughts and pestilence, but God's perfect gardening skills now provided a bountiful harvest. Tim and I made a deliberate choice to believe that God is a God of the impossible and that He could give Tim a wonderful job— no matter what his age or his credentials, and no matter how long he was unemployed. When the right time came, God not only provided Tim with a job, but one that allowed him to earn a good living.

Several days after Tim began working, we found the house that we wanted to purchase. "We need to have settlement by mid-December so our family can be together for Christmas," Tim told our realtor. That only gave us three weeks to procure a mortgage and settle on the house. It might have seemed impossible to do, but with our family's expertly pruned faith, we knew that *with God, all things are possible* (Matthew 19:26). We placed our desires firmly in God's hands, and we *expected* Him to do what He knew was best for us.

We settled on December tenth, and the movers arrived with our possessions on the fifteenth. One of the first things I unpacked was the notebook with my wish lists for our next house and Tim's next job. I poured a cup of coffee and slowly read through both lists, realizing that God provided almost every wish on my carefully-assembled lists.

Tim, our children Justin and Megan, and I celebrated Christmas in a house of our own for the first time in two years. Sitting together at our kitchen table on Christmas Day, Megan asked me a question. "Mom, can we really expect God to answer prayers?"

I immediately recognized that this was the moment Reverend Kate had foreseen nearly two years before. I retrieved my notebook.

"Right after Dad and I moved in with Aunt Emma, Reverend Kate called me. She told me to envision our blessing by drawing up detailed lists of everything I wanted in Dad's new job and our new house. You've been in every room, so you'll know if God answered my prayers."

I opened the notebook to the page with my house wish list. "The first item is a two-car garage." I looked at Justin and Megan to see if they recognized that God provided that request and both nodded affirmatively.

"With dry-wall." Megan and Justin's eyes opened wide, and my voice quivered. "And painted."

When I reached the end of the list, I asked my children to tell me if we can expect God to answer our prayers. Justin whispered, "Yes," but Megan couldn't reply. She wiped her eyes with her sleeve.

"Justin? Megan?"

"Yes, Mom?"

"Just wait till I read the list for your dad's new job."

Names have been changed.

TIME TO REFLECT ON GOD'S PROVISION

Help my complaining spirit, Lord, when my life becomes
uncomfortable. Help me remember You gave up
Your home in heaven for me.

Do not store up for yourselves treasures on earth,
where moth and rust destroy,
and where thieves break in and steal.

—Matthew 6:19 (NIV 1984)

20

HUMILITY
Felicia Bowen Bridges

I beseech you therefore, brethren, by the mercies of God,
that you present your bodies a living sacrifice,
holy, acceptable to God, which is your reasonable service.
—Romans 12:1 (NKJV)

My husband and I spent our first fifteen years of marriage successfully pursuing the American Dream. On our fifteenth anniversary that dream changed forever. After building a six-figure income in computer marketing, a job loss forced us to start over. My husband had worked for a major company, so I found myself surprised when he took a job selling clothing at a department store.

The hardest part of this new journey was leaving our beloved house. It was my dream house—the epitome of everything we'd worked toward for fifteen years.

I remember when we decided to build our home. I spent nearly two years looking at every new neighborhood in a 20-mile radius and finally settled on one. I then looked at floor plans until my eyes crossed. I imagined what each plan looked like as I walked through the house in my mind. Eventually, I selected the perfect plan for our family. It had four bedrooms, a huge open kitchen and a great room, formal dining and living rooms, and an unfinished basement and garage—complete with rough-ins for a bathroom, so we could turn it into an in-law suite, should the need arise.

I checked the builder's progress daily for six months as my dream became a reality. I poured over carpet samples, paint swatches, and light fixtures, selecting each one with the sure knowledge that this would be our home until our kids were grown and gone. It would be the home they would return to with their families when we were old and gray. The home they would recall in their fondest memories of childhood.

Even to me, this reads as if my heart was set on worldly things, but my sincere desire for the house was to glorify God. I sought the Lord often throughout the building process. I offered time and again to lay this house on the altar if it was not in His will. I promised that if it was His will, it would be given back to Him in every way I could imagine.

God provided the house, and we gave Him all the glory and tried to be good stewards, using the home to host traveling missionaries and families in dire straits. The large, spacious rooms hosted weekly Bible studies, birthday parties, family and Sunday school gatherings, and progressive dinners. We built strong relationships with our neighbors, reaching out to show them the love of Christ and ministering to them at every opportunity.

Eventually, the remembrance of my promise to lay it on the altar faded.

It was on our fifteenth anniversary that we got the news. I was walking to my car after helping out in my son's kindergarten classroom when my cell phone rang.

"I'm being laid off," Randy said without preamble. It wasn't entirely unexpected. With regular off-shoring and down-sizing, lay-offs had become a regular occurrence. We had also sensed that God was calling us to walk away from the corporate lifestyle, calling Randy into full-time ministry. He was taking evening classes at Seminary with a goal of eventually earning a Master of Divinity in Church Music. But with four children and a "certain standard of living to maintain," we hadn't found the right time to make the transition.

Apparently, the "right time" had come.

Randy was the sole breadwinner for nearly our entire marriage. From the time our daughter was born twelve years prior, I was a stay-at-home mom. It wasn't always easy, but we were confident that our children needed me at home until they began school, at least. Our youngest was three years old.

We comforted and encouraged one another that God had a plan. Randy had been serving as interim Music Minister for several months, after his dear friend and mentor had been called to a church in his home state. Perhaps the layoff was God's way of opening the opportunity for Randy to begin serving vocationally. We eagerly prayed for God to show us His plan.

Sixteen days after news of the layoff, I received another life-changing call.

Randy's mother was struggling through chemotherapy and radiation treatments for pancreatic cancer. The treatments left Faye weak, often barely able to get out of bed. Earlier that week, she'd missed an appointment because she and John simply slept through it. Randy was furious with his father for the oversight; he scolded him for not being more responsible about her care. But by Thursday evening he had calmed down and knew he needed to forgive his dad and ask forgiveness for his harsh words. Thankfully, it was Fall Break at seminary, so Randy was not in class and was able to call his dad and make amends.

The next morning, a friend invited Randy out for a rare round of golf to encourage him.

It was a little past noon when our phone rang. Faye's voice quavered as she asked for her oldest son. When I told her he was playing golf, but should be home soon, she said, "John is asleep and I can't wake him up."

John typically rose before the sun to walk their dogs and fix breakfast, but would often nap in the recliner. I asked if that's what he was doing.

"No, he's still in the bed."

I knew immediately. I told her I would call Randy's cell phone and he would be there shortly, but that she should call 911.

As a result of the layoff, Randy golfed just ten minutes from their home—instead of sitting in an office an hour away—and pulled into the driveway as the EMS team arrived. Within minutes, they confirmed what I had known—John had passed away from a sudden heart attack while he slept.

For ten months we had prepared our hearts for the possibility that his mother would not survive the inoperable cancer in her pancreas. We had worried over his father and wondered how he would manage without her. Instead, we faced his funeral and the question of how to care for her through this illness.

I can't even begin to list all the miracles that surrounded us during this time, but God made it clear that there are no accidents, no coincidences. His hand was there constantly: lifting us, comforting us, carrying us through the next seven months.

In the midst of all this turmoil and tragedy, God whispered a calling to our oldest daughter. Our church was sponsoring a mission trip to Prague, Czech Republic, led by our pastor, a native Czech. At age twelve, it seemed premature, illogical, impractical, and financially impossible, yet God made it clear that she and I were to join this mission team. We committed to raise almost $4,000 within weeks of Randy's layoff. Uncertain of why, we submitted ourselves to His call. God provided every cent needed for the trip—even our spending money—without us needing to use any money intended for bills.

As the trip drew near, I grew concerned about Faye's condition. She was frail and delicate. She'd moved into our home so I could help care for her during the day, and I worried about leaving her alone—even to shop for groceries. I prayed that she would be all right while Megan and I were on the mission trip. My heart ached over the thought that she might pass away while we were gone and I would not be there for Randy. In God's sovereignty, Faye joined John to worship around the throne of the King a month before the mission trip.

Randy took a job in the men's department at Dillard's. After taxes, his check barely covered our grocery bill and was less than he would have received for unemployment, but it gave him peace of mind and a sense of self-worth that standing in the unemployment line would have ravaged.

Megan and I returned from Prague with a new sense of priorities. Nothing brings the bountiful blessings of living in America into sharper focus than visiting another country. With a new perspective on the necessities of life, God brought to mind my promise to lay our home on the altar of His will.

We had survived for eight months on severance pay, frugality, and Randy's meager income from Dillard's. With our resources dwindling and the added financial burden of half of his parents' mortgage payment, we knew something had to change.

We considered selling his parents' home, but it was barely worth what was owed and was in need of maintenance due to the months of neglect since John passed away. Our home, however, had appreciated nicely, in addition to the down payment we had made. It occurred to me that, despite the tragedy of losing John and Faye so close together, God was providing the means for us to downsize without having to qualify for a mortgage on Randy's new retail income. In addition, my in-laws' home was ten minutes from the Seminary and no farther from the children's school than our current home.

I suggested this solution to Randy, but he was adamant that we stay in the home God provided. We trimmed expenses and calculated how we might keep the house if he took on the full-time ministry position in addition to his job at Dillard's.

God often closes the door on good and better to lead us to His best.

We served actively as members of our church for eleven years. Randy served as a deacon, apprenticed under the music minister for seven years, and volunteered to handle his duties when he resigned. After serving in this role for six months on a part-time basis, the church leadership asked him to accept the position, pending a vote by the membership. It seemed, at least to our eyes, like a natural progression. But when church members requested Randy's resume to evaluate his qualifications to serve as music minister and others leapt to his defense, it was clear that God had closed this door. Randy removed his name from consideration. Whatever the cost to us, we could not allow his ministry to become a source of conflict within the body of Christ.

God called us to make a move, break out of our comfort zone, and take an Abram-style journey. Christ was calling us to leave everything to follow Him.

We put our house on the market and it sold within a week. After identifying the furniture that could fit in his parents' home, we sold the rest and were settled in our "new" home in three weeks.

Within three weeks of moving, Randy was called to serve bi-vocationally as music minister at another church.

God pried our fingers away from everything we clung to, aside from Him. Any worldly notion we found security in, He ripped from our hands. It hurt. Parting with the antique dining room set I'd grown up with, a gift from my parents when we'd moved into the house, was almost as difficult as saying goodbye to my dream home. Even our marriage itself was tested and refined as through fire.

We often mistakenly define humility as having a poor perception of our self-worth, but it is really having an accurate assessment of our worth in God's sight and a willingness to allow God, who created us and knows best our strengths and talents, to direct our paths.

His plan is perfect, even when it doesn't make sense to us. Although the mission trip to Prague seemed foolish to many, it planted a missionary heart in our daughter that is growing and bursting with fruit as she prepares to return to Prague as a missionary after her college graduation.

Reminiscing on what God accomplished in our hearts and lives during this journey brings such joy. God is enough. When we lose our jobs, He is enough. When we lose our homes, He is enough. When friends desert us, He is enough. When everything else is gone, He is still enough.

TIME TO REFLECT ON GOD'S PROVISION

There is no joy like the joy in knowing I am
right in the center of Your perfect will.

*You will seek Me and find Me when
you seek Me with all your heart.*
—Jeremiah 29:13 (NIV)

21

RECOVERING FROM A LOST CALL
Roger E. Bruner

There are different kinds of gifts, but the same
Spirit distributes them.
There are different kinds of service, but the same Lord.
There are different kinds of working,
but in all of them and in everyone it is the same God at work.

—1 Corinthians 12: 4-6 (NIV)

They say a man loses more than just his income when he loses his job; he loses a major part of his identity. I believe that's true. I lost more than that, however. When I lost my job at the International Mission Board, I lost my calling. I couldn't avoid wondering whether God would ever help me recover from a loss that great.

I grew up the only child of a Baptist minister. From earliest childhood, I believed pastors and missionaries—and everyone else in a full-time Christian vocation—were special. God chose them; He called them to be His servants. Yet I also saw what life had been like for my parents. We lived in parsonages that came nowhere close to the quality of housing most of our church members enjoyed, and we could never afford many of the little things other people took for granted. I not only resented those sacrifices, I prayed in my own selfish way that—whatever God chose to do with me—He wouldn't call me into a full-time Christian vocation. Anything but that.

I didn't have any real sense of calling when I taught ninth-grade English for six-plus years and even less when I worked as a job counselor/interviewer for almost ten. My aging parents knew I hadn't found my niche—or should I say God hadn't revealed it yet?—and they offered to pay for my study of computer programming at a local community college. They thought I might enjoy and benefit from it, and they were right. I had never caught on to anything so easily. Programming was definitely going to be my "thing." After all those years, had God finally led me to the right something?

You know the old adage about not being able to get a job without first having experience? That proved true even in a field that was wide open at the time. I had always been interested in the Foreign Mission Board of the Southern Baptist Convention. My family had historical connections to it, and it was located in Richmond, Virginia, where my parents lived. Two big pluses. Through a series of minor miracles—God was working this out His way in His time, even though I couldn't see it yet—the human resources director's response to my continuing interest changed remarkably quickly from, "We only hire people with experience," to "We've got something in-house now that's so new we can't find enough experienced people."

From my initial interview with him to a luncheon interview with the heads of the tiny Information Technology department, I felt as if God was about to deliver me to the Promised Land. I was going to find the home I'd spent over sixteen years wandering in the work wilderness searching for. Something I truly felt called to. I waited for the job offer. It didn't come. I grew impatient. Too often, I reminded the human resources director of my continued interest—and never received a response. I reminded God even more frequently, but He remained equally silent. While on vacation with my in-laws that summer I felt pushed to look for a programming job in that area—an area far from Richmond. My heart wasn't there, however. I clearly belonged at the Foreign Mission Board—even if they didn't know it yet—and I wasn't going to compromise.

One day, I flopped down on the bed in frustration and prayed one of the sincerest prayers I've ever prayed. *Lord, I can't make anything happen. It's all in Your hands. Please do whatever You want to.* Not two days later, I heard from my parents. The Foreign Mission Board had been looking for me, and I was to call as soon as I got home. Finally! I'd received not just a physical call, but—more important—a spiritual one. God knew I didn't have the temperament to be a pastor or a missionary, but He also knew I was just right for working behind the scenes at an agency that recruited and trained, sent and supported missionaries throughout the world. Not to mention keeping Southern Baptists fired up about the importance of missions. I was set. I relished

my work and took advantage of every opportunity to become
more immersed in missions. I did everything from attending
the weekly chapel service to playing bass guitar at International
Mission Board (the Foreign Mission Board's current name)
events at the Lifeway Conference Centers at Glorieta, New
Mexico and Ridgecrest, North Carolina. I most enjoyed going on
numerous volunteer mission trips to Romania, England, Wales,
and Australia.

After eighteen satisfying years at the International Mission
Board, things changed. We transitioned from mainframe
computers to personal computers and started looking for new
ways to use the Internet. Although I thought I was keeping up
with the changes, I soon learned—in a most unpleasant way—
how wrong I was. My department director asked me—I could tell
from his tone I had to say yes, no matter how I felt—whether I
would transfer to a different team. I agreed. Reluctantly.

Try as I might, I never adjusted to my new assignment. I made
some major mistakes, my performance slipped dangerously, and
I couldn't have felt more miserable or useless. One day—a year
or so into this role I'd proven incapable of handling—I arrived at
work and found everyone sitting around, looking gloomy, and
discussing a newspaper article about a pending downsizing at the
International Mission Board. Considering my lack of success over
the past year, I knew that if a downsizing took place, I of all
people didn't *deserve* to stay.

I was one of the sixty-some people laid off that day. On one
hand, I felt elated—or at least relieved—to be free of the biggest
failure of my life. On the other—it took a while for the reality to

kick in—I had lost the call it had taken so many years to receive. I would no longer be serving God in the way that had been so special for almost nineteen years and the way I'd expected to serve until retirement and beyond (as a volunteer).

At first, income wasn't an issue. Not only had the International Mission Board provided months of salary and insurance benefits, they allowed me to convert a number of unused vacation days to cash. Nonetheless, I felt like a non-swimmer someone had just thrown into the middle of a turbulent ocean. Maybe I couldn't see sharks, but neither did I feel the comfort of a sandy bottom beneath my feet or see dry land a few quick strokes away.

The search for a new call from God seemed irrelevant; I'd lost the one that really mattered. So I threw myself into the task of finding a new job. The mission board paid for special job search classes. I bought a suit—the first one I'd owned in years. I ordered some business cards. I whipped my resume into the best shape it had ever been in.

Even though I gained the job-seeking skills I needed, something was missing. My call. There was only one International Mission Board. God had brought me there. Why hadn't He let me stay? Bit by bit, He helped me realize He'd been gently urging me to move on. But I'd been too committed to my previous call to listen. He knew this downsizing was the only way to get my attention.

Okay, Lord, I'm listening. What do you want me to do? I'm not old enough to retire, but Information Technology has worn me out. It's changing so rapidly I don't think I have the energy or the patience to keep up with it any longer.

God answered by involving me in several job search groups. One met at a Bob Evans restaurant, where the weekly fellowship time was more meaningful than the leads discussed. Another took place at the Needle's Eye Ministries headquarters. Both of those groups were Christ-centered. A third group—a secular one—met in the public room of a local grocery store.

It was at these meetings that I came to appreciate how pastors and missionaries must feel when they must quit doing what God once called them to do and move on to something else. I kept asking God, "What do I want to do 'when I grow up'? Moreover, what do *You* want me to do?" I was back at square one.

God then inspired me to write a song I dedicated to my Bob Evans group. I often sang it to myself for encouragement:

I believe God's working behind the scenes;
He's helping me in ways I can't see.
God understands all my problems;
He knows my best efforts are not enough to solve them.
I believe God's working behind the scenes;
He's retouching my faded hopes and dreams.
God always provides the things He knows I need.
I believe God's holding me in His hands,
Assuring me I'm safe in His plans.
God banishes fear and confusion;
I know that His way is the only true solution.
I believe God's working behind the scenes,
Drawing from His unlimited means.
God always provides the things He knows I need.

I believe God's working behind the scenes;
He's retouching my faded hopes and dreams.
God always provides the things He knows I need.

I felt very strongly that God was in control. He *had* to be. I sure wasn't. Few normal people *enjoy* life's bad times. Yet this time of seeking brought me closer to God than ever before. My prayer times were more personal and more special than before. That turned the pain and uncertainty into a blessing. God had never let me down, and I knew He would get me through my job search. Not only would He provide income again, He would open the door to job fulfillment.

My faith was stronger than my patience, however. I was tired of looking for work and I was tired of waiting. Two jobs later, I ended up working at a Target store up the road from me, where I remained for three years. I could have griped to God about how useless my education and former *professional* employment history seemed then, but instead I thanked Him for a far less-stressful job than any of my previous ones. Although I hadn't recovered from my lost call, at least I was doing the biblically honorable thing: working.

My hours at Target were part-time, though, and I felt a strong urge to use my off-hours as productively as possible. God had given me that time for a reason, and He didn't want me to waste it. For years I had wanted to write a novel, but I'd never had a good idea. Nor a bad one. I'd mentally shelved that goal until retirement. God had something else in mind, though. He gave me a great idea and helped me write my first novel, even though my wife and I probably got a little ahead of His plans by self-publishing it.

Once I consumed writing books by the dozen and attended Christian writing conferences, I realized that the first book wasn't nearly as good as I'd thought. Or as good as God knew I was capable of writing. Nonetheless, that first novel convinced me that God had given me a talent for writing Christian fiction. I would use that talent for *His* glory, not mine. So I kept writing, studying, and working to improve my writing, as well as praying for God to use my manuscripts in whatever way He chose.

Boy, was He ever more in charge of what took place after that! My wife believed so strongly in my writing that we agreed I should retire at sixty-two to write full-time. And an acquisitions editor at a publishing company that didn't publish novels like mine liked my writing so much she sent one of my manuscripts to a literary agent who agreed it needed to be in print. He signed me without my having to do anything. That led to the publication of my first two books. I have a contract for a third now, and the future is where it belongs—in God's hands. Right where it's been all along, even when I couldn't see where I was headed.

God keeps working in my life. He's helped me recover from one lost call by calling me to something more special than I'd ever dreamed of. I pray that I'll write what He wants me to write and use my new call to reach out in His name to others through my words. And to touch my readers—past, present, and future—in a way that pleases Him. That's ultimate job satisfaction.

Time to Reflect on God's Provision

"It's not the house that makes the home. We make the home."
–Nadine Roland

Lord, help me find my worth, not in material things,
but in You alone.

22

WHERE ARE WE GOING?
La-Tan Roland Murphy

But you will not leave in haste or go in flight;
for the LORD will go before you,
the God of Israel will be your rear guard.
—Isaiah 52:12 (NIV)

"Where are we going? Why are we leaving?" I asked my husband as we backed out of our driveway.

"Trust me," he gently said, cutting his big, green eyes my way, a sneaky grin spreading across his handsome face.

"Seriously, honey, where are we going?"

"You will know where we are going and why we are going when we get there," he said again, with a flirtatious chuckle.

My husband's job had always been secure, but when his company merged and they hired new upper management, the political games began. With so much transition going on in the company, many people were laid off, and the remaining employees were stressed and concerned, knowing they could be the next person fired. Many employees voluntarily resigned, looking for greener pastures. When my husband came home from the office, he had trouble unwinding from the stressful conditions he was forced to work under. The tension on his face said it all.

My husband sensed his job was threatened but had no clear proof—only his intuition. He had enjoyed many years of good standing with the original corporate executives. They greatly respected him as a professional and often consulted with him on special projects. When the merging company took control of the company's board, my husband's boss, Mr. Thomas,* aligned with the new chief executive officer. This was a detriment to my husband's well-standing position in the company. All former executives and upper management were victims of the toxic political games. This caused distrust amongst the team. The integrity that had drawn my husband to accept his position in this company no longer existed as the cut-throat mentality created a stress-filled environment.

Each day, I watched the decline in my husband's motivation and drive. As his stress and the fear of a potential job loss mounted, he slowly became a dead man walking. With only the president remaining from the original executive team, my husband felt alone and had no support system left. He had no confidence in his boss, because he'd witnessed first-hand the demonstrated lack of integrity. He struggled most when he discovered lies were used to manipulate and add pressure to other employees who already feared losing their jobs. Trust was broken on all accounts. Being a man of integrity, my husband called the lies out of darkness and into the light when they were told. This fueled the fire between him and his boss and frustrations mounted. Being the sole provider for our family of five added more pressure to my husband's already stress-filled days as he quietly contemplated where to go next.

It was so painful watching my husband go from a confident professional who enjoyed the fruit of his work to a worn-down man who felt trapped in a prison. His confidence had been beaten into the ground, and he questioned if he could find another job that would pay what he currently made. These doubts held him hostage, and there was a point at which I worried about the toll the stress took on his health. On two occasions, he ended up in the emergency room with chest pain.

We began to pray for God to provide strength and direction.

One day, my husband's boss brought a new hire into his office. This came as quite a shock, since there had been no announcement that my husband would be reporting to someone else. Amazingly, my husband's new manager was a godly man and former fellow church member of ours. My husband knew God was working for his good and leading the stressful work situation in a new direction, having brought Mr. Lewis* there.

The Lord began to use the new manager to confirm my husband's worth and reiterate his value to the company. Because Mr. Lewis was a godly man, he would have no part in the political games being played. Every decision he made was based on integrity and honesty. He spoke up where truth needed to be spoken and would not back down when he encountered injustice. Mr. Lewis also interceded for my husband when his job was in jeopardy. Because my husband had good standing with the original company's last remaining top executive, Mr. Thomas knew he could not fire my husband without valid reasons.

One day, Mr. Lewis took my husband out to lunch and gave warning of the plan to eliminate his job. This was part of Mr. Thomas' political ploy to force my husband to resign. Mr. Lewis told my husband that he disagreed with the decision and found no fault in him. He could only protect him for so long. He spoke words of confidence over my husband and complimented his work, saying he found it to be exceptional. He didn't want my husband to be caught off guard and left unprepared for what was to come.

This preluded a series of events that would lead my husband away from this company. Though left completely vulnerable, there was nothing more my husband could do but turn to the God of his childhood and cling to the faith his parents had demonstrated through the years. We felt like the Israelites when they left Egypt, not knowing where we were going or what we were going to do. While Egypt was not the best situation, the Israelites had become tolerant of their harsh circumstances. When Moses led them out, they didn't know where they were going. They had no choice but to put their trust in Moses' ability to lead them to the Promised Land. My husband's godly manager, Mr. Lewis, told him he was much more valuable than management made him feel, and that God had a better plan for him than to be held in bondage—unappreciated at this company.

It was not long after this that Mr. Lewis was fired, because he refused to follow the politics or be manipulated for the sake of political gain. God had clearly brought him to the company—though for a short time—for the sake of supporting my husband, confirming his value and worth during a time when he desperately needed it. Through every emotional up and down, God was there taking care of my husband by placing not just anyone in the position as management over him, but a godly man who would represent him well. God had proven Himself to be the Almighty rear guard. He lovingly guarded my husband's back when he felt like he was against the wall.

Like the Israelites, who toughed it out and stayed in bondage for more years than expected, my husband had stayed past his appointed time. It was time to walk toward the exit door.

This started a slow, downward spiral leading to a financially dry, desert place. Like the Israelites, we initially found excitement in leaving the prison and bondage of our Egypt. We wondered where God would take us.

Through the years that followed, God led us slowly from one point to another. Each point of our journey taught us something new, ultimately steadying our faith and trust in Him as the Great Provider. Looking back we realized that although not every business endeavor was a blessed one, each one was a stepping stone to where we are today. We often questioned why we could not have just left the bondage of Egypt and gone straight to the Promised Land. Why we had to go through the financial despair desert at all was a lingering question haunting our minds, but we knew beyond a shadow of doubt that God Himself had sifted all the events of our lives through His mighty hands. He certainly would not waste one thing and would show us His power through each devastating blow if we remained consistent and kept walking.

There were multiple roadblocks along the way. We stumbled over many of them, but as our faith grew, the same stumbling blocks suddenly became stepping-stones leading to God's desired best for our lives. Several years later, God led us to a business partner who is a man of deep godly character. The work relationship between him and my husband is one based on the principles of God's word. What a blessing it is to work with a man of such character and faith. He and his wife truly exhibit servant hearts in every sense. Their lives are defined by giving. There are no hidden agendas or selfish motives. Every decision made in their business is based on integrity. There are many companies who put the word integrity in their company mission statements but few who would put a word like integrity within their company name. This is how important it is to my husband's current business partner that all their customers know what their lives are defined by, both personally and in the business world.

We came to realize it was through the desert places we depended on God the most. When all pride-filled self-reliance was stripped away, we were able to see our need for God's redirecting power in our lives. Once we leaned completely on Him and trusted Him with all of our hearts, souls, minds, and strength to provide for us in each tough time, our faith grew and was strengthened deeply. We knew and understood beyond all logic where our source of help came from. Had we been allowed to go directly into the blessed Promised Land of financial peace and prosperity, we may have prided ourselves into thinking we had reached it in our own strength. Perhaps we would have failed to give God the glory He so deserved, or perhaps we would not have even acknowledged His faithful hand of provision at all.

God's provision in all of our lives represents so many things. At times, His provision comes in the form of a trusted godly person who speaks into us. At times, He provides only our basic needs for each day in order to show us His promises are true. At times, He provides unique journeys that act as part of a greater surprise He wants to lead us to. We must trust Him and be surrendered to His leading if we want to experience the Promised Land.

In comparison to the trials most of us face each day, today *is* the Promised Land. Our Promised Land is not based solely on monetary prosperity but on living uprightly before our God, who has been with us every step of our journey thus far—whether we choose to recognize His presence on the journey or not.

These days, the motives of my husband and I are far different and our lives are defined by God's leading. We are slowly rebuilding our lives financially, and in many ways we have started over completely. But there is peace in knowing we are choosing to do the journey God's way.

On the day my husband told me to come with him on a surprise journey, I wanted to know where we were going. I resisted because I wasn't sure I was prepared for the trip. In much the same way, God is trying to lead each of His children to new places, but we are too busy questioning where He is taking us instead of trusting His good plan for our life's journey. We can be sure He is taking us to better places than we can conceive. As long as He knows where we are going, why should we hesitate or resist going with Him?

We do not need to have all the answers right away. Like my husband said to me, "You will know where you are going and why you are going when we get there." There is no peace like the peace that passes all understanding we will receive when we allow God to lead us every step of the way. He will carry us through every tough time we will ever face.

My husband and I are so thankful God's provisional leadership was with us, even when we did not know where we were going or why we had to leave.

Names have been changed.

Time to Reflect on God's Provision

Every part of my life seemed to be coming undone.
But when I was flat on my back, there was
only one place to look—
UP!
It was then I realized I was still breathing;
I would survive this financial despair.

He is before all things and in Him all things hold together.
—Colossians 1:17 (NIV)

23

SHE CRIES ON SATURDAYS
Eddie Jones

Saturday, Feb. 5, 2011—Eddie's Prayer Journal
*Lord, we're giving up Bennie's car today. May your Grace be
with us. May your power be made perfect in our grief …
and in my failure as a husband.*

God provides—but not as we hope and not in our time. For years I wanted to write a book called *God is Good, God is Great, God is Slow but Never Late.* I am still waiting for him to give me the words behind the title. Perhaps these last fifteen years are chapters in that book.

In May of 1997, an employment headhunter called during dinner. We never answer the phone during dinner—or, at least we didn't before cell phones. Back then, dinner was family time—those few minutes when our boys argued, refused to eat, my wife sulked, and I kept my head bowed while I shoveled in food. The boys no longer live with us. Now my wife and I eat from TV trays, speak too little, and watch lousy television shows. But in

May of 1997, I felt compelled to answer the phone. Turns out God called that evening.

"Can you be at IBM at 9:45 tomorrow morning? I have a job interview lined up for you."

The headhunter spoke with a thick New York accent. I felt sure the call was a scam. I said as much and asked what he wanted, why he was calling me, and how much this "interview" would cost me. Joe assured me the meeting was a legit interview, that my resume had landed on his desk and IBM needed web programmers.

I skipped a few sales calls the next morning and drove to IBM's main building in the Research Triangle Park. The interview lasted fifteen minutes. The head of the department spent most of our time on the phone. I sat across from him reviewing web code printed out on a sheet of paper. I recognized maybe 10 percent of the markup language. The truth was, I had no business claiming to be an "HTML Editor." I had learned some HTML tags by looking at the source code of web pages and making changes to the letters. The only reason I put "HTML Editor" on my resume was because I wanted to be a full-time writer and I figured "editor" would look good on my list of skills.

The department head hung up and looked at me from across his desk. "Any questions?"

I shook my head, we chatted a little about IBM, and I left. While driving to my sales job (I sold toilet paper), I remained convinced the only reason IBM called me in for an interview was to fill a quota. I figured the job would be filled in-house and they had to post and interview a certain number of candidates. I fit into their "loser candidate" folder.

That night, the headhunter called to tell me IBM wanted to offer me a contract with their PC division. It turns out, in 1997 IBM still sent all their web updates to Ogilvy and Mather, a New York ad firm. A simple text change on a web page cost IBM over a hundred dollars. To save money, CEO Lou Gerstner demanded the PC division bring basic web maintenance duties in-house. I was their first contract hire.

My friend Dale reminded me later that God loved me so much He created the Internet just so I would have a job. All I know is the first morning I drove to IBM, I felt terrified and relieved God had provided a new job. For two years I had prayed for him to find me work in another field—and now He had.

God is good. *My grace is sufficient for you, for My power is made perfect in weakness* (2 Corinthians 12:9 NIV).

Saturday, Feb. 5, 2011—Eddie's Prayer Journal
Lord, CarMax is redeeming Bennie's car. I beg you, redeem us. We need a financial miracle.

I remained at IBM for seven years. Then, in 2004, they sent my job to India. I could have (maybe) remained in project management, but I'm an ideas guy. Details bore me. When I told my wife IBM had let me go, she cried. I told her not to worry, that God would provide. After all, He'd created the web so I could work at IBM. Surely He had something better planned for us.

We banked my severance pay, I created a new resume, and we filed for unemployment. Though my wife pushed me to apply for IT positions with other companies, I found the idea depressing. I had worked for one of the world's largest companies. If I could not find security there, where would I? I knew the only real security lay in working for God. With His help and my wife's reluctant encouragement, I started my own web business.

For five years, I ran a small web company. During my best year I earned half of what I'd made at IBM. My wife and I stopped saving for our future and gave up shopping for each other. We cut out restaurants, vacations, and let repairs on our home slide. My wife continued driving our minivan. I inherited a "beater car" from a friend. (A beater car is a car too beat up to sell and too good to junk.)

A year after leaving IBM, I attended my first writers' conference. God spoke to me, and with the help of my friend Cindy Sproles, we launched Christian Devotions Ministries in 2007. More time passed. The labor pains of the Great Recession rumbled through the economy, and one spring, at the close of the Blue Ridge Mountains Christian Writers Conference, my friend Ann Tatlock looked at me from across the table and said, "So, when are you going to quit your job and do this full-time?"

She meant write. She meant run the ministry. She meant step out in faith. When God speaks, we have two choices. We can turn back or advance.

I knew what lay behind and there was no future there. I left the conference and listed my business for sale. That summer, under the willow tree in my yard, I signed a sheet of paper telling

God I would do whatever He asked; that in working for Him I knew I would have job security. Based on what I'd read in the Bible, God seemed like a fair boss. Those who received talents and worked hard received more work and opportunity. I agreed to trust God completely that He would provide for our needs. In 2009, I sold my web business and began writing full-time and growing Christian Devotions Ministries.

God is Great. *When you pass through the waters, I will be with you; and when you pass through the rivers, they will not sweep over you. When you walk through the fire, you will not be burned; the flames will not set you ablaze* (Isaiah 43:2 NIV).

Thursday, Feb. 10, 2011—Eddie's Prayer Journal
Lord, I don't feel like I'm using my talents fully, but foolishly. Help me to know how to invest your talents so they will return a good harvest. Help me bless others through the use of my gifts.

Two months after I sold my web business, I landed a ghost-writing project that provided income for six months. After that project ended, another smaller project arrived. I followed the advice of friends and applied for freelance work, subscribed to "freelance work lists," and marketed my skills. Not once did I land any paying work in this way. I slowly learned to heed the voice of the Spirit. What works for one man will not work for another. We must wear the armor God provides for each of us.

The ministry grew, my writing opportunities expanded (through small miracles), and I continued to believe that large book contract lay just around the corner. When the big contract did not appear, I signed with small houses that liked my writing but had limited marketing experience. And still, I worked with writers and authors, encouraging them to write the story God placed on their heart. Christian Devotions Ministries grew. My ministry partner and I began teaching at writers conferences. We began publishing books for other authors. In short, we did what we could to help others, even as our own income dwindled.

The summer of 2010, our new friends Jeff and Rebecca invited us to Washington State for a summer vacation. They provided our plane tickets and put us up for the week. This was a trip we could not afford. My wife loved it; she needed it. For a few days, the stress of worrying about how she would pay the bills subsided. But I knew that when we returned home, there would be no income. All of my writing leads had dried up. By the end of July, we would be out of money.

On the Fourth of July, while watching fireworks explode over Seattle, I received an email from a business partner. For several years, I had helped run a boating website. We had tried to sell the business several times but failed. He wrote with an ultimatum: I could accept his buyout offer so he could have full ownership or see my role and income reduced. I looked at the email and smiled.

While waiting in the Spokane airport to catch our flight home, I told my wife about the offer. My portion of the buyout would give us income for one year. I would have to write fast and pray for God's blessing on my novels. I accepted the offer and another door closed. From now on, all my income would come from work in God's kingdom.

God is Slow. *Do not fear, for I have redeemed you. I have summoned you by name; you are mine* (Isaiah 43:1 NIV).

Tuesday, Feb. 08, 2011—Eddie's Prayer Journal
Lord, help me to release my dreams—whatever that means. Help me to see past my failures and see INTO Your face. You created the dream. You gave it to me. Do not let me sow it with sin. Let me give it back to You and trust You to do what is best.

Christmas 2010 arrived. I sold a vintage Hobie surfboard gathering dust in the crawl space of our home. The $800 provided funds for Christmas gifts. By now we were living on a tight budget with my wife forecasting the months when the money would be gone. My first novel, *The Curse of Captain LaFoote,* released. I expected big things. The sales did not materialize. The book has since won a couple of awards, but it has never provided so much as a decent meal for my family. This is the reality of a novelist and the reason they call us starving artists. In January, after the boys were back at college and the trappings of Christmas stuffed into trash barrels, my wife asked, "How much longer will we have to live like this?"

I did not know. I knew God … but beyond that I knew nothing about our future. Only that a God of love would not let His people starve. He never had—at least not in Scripture when they lived in obedience to His Word.

But Never Late. *Well done … I will put you in charge of many things* (Matthew 25:21 NIV).

Tuesday, Feb. 08, 2011—Eddie's Prayer Journal
*Lord, have we been stingy to You? I feel like I have given my life to
You. And yet, the riches haven't been returned. So I am asking: Do I
need to do more? The ministry is broke—we're broke!
So tell me, tell us. What do we do next?*

On Saturday, February 5, 2011, we sold my wife's car to
CarMax. This was her dream car, the black CRV with leather
seats. Her first new car just for her. We could no longer afford the
$450 car payment. Praise God, we received more money than we
owed. But as the two of us walked across the parking lot toward
our old van, my wife laid her head on my shoulder and cried.

Cried over a car. Cried over the fact that at our age, after all
our years of working hard, going to church, praying, and trying so
hard to do the right thing, we could not hang on to our dreams.
Part of it may have been my wife remembering her dad. He had
passed away six months earlier. He would not have let her lose the
car. But he was gone, and now her car was too.

The next Saturday, we purchased new tires for the old van.
She cried on the way home. There was nothing I could do as a
husband to fix her broken heart or our broken finances. I had
heard God's voice—was sure of it. I had advanced and forced
those I loved to advance with me. Now the consequences of
walking with and trusting fully in God had brought us to a spirit
of brokenness.

The summer of 2011, we sold the old van and bought a used
Hyundai Santa Fe—a "poor mom's" Honda. We remain a one-car

family. By then I had begun to suspect what God was doing in our lives—in the life of my wife.

"Your dad is dead, and I'm sorry," I said to her in my prayers. "I know you miss him. I miss him. And I know our boys miss him. But your father was your god. As long as he lived, you knew help would come, no matter what. But God is asking you to trust *Him* in that same way you trusted your dad. Your heavenly Father wants you to believe *He* will keep your foot from falling. Our finances are but one test. The next test will not be a car, but possibly our house, a child, or our health. If we cannot trust God for transportation on earth, how will we ever trust Him to transport us to His throne?"

Our financial burden has lessened. Turns out writing for God can pay pretty well. But my wife still cries—if not on Saturdays, then on other days.

We have not missed a meal or missed a house or utility payment. But we have, both of us, misused our God-given talents. We squandered years working for the security of a paycheck and savings, and in the end we learned only God can be trusted. He promised to provide for our daily needs, not our monthly needs or retirement years.

When will the next royalty check arrive? I don't know. I only know this: God is never late.

Time To Reflect On God's Provision

"When will the stress end?"
I must have cried out to God a million times,
asking Him the same question.

Trust in the Lord with all your heart and lean not on
your own understanding;
in all your ways acknowledge Him,
and He will make your paths straight.

—Proverbs 3:5-6 (NIV 1984)

24

LIFE ON THE LAUGH FRONTIER
Torry Martin

Have I not commanded you? Be strong and courageous.
Do not be terrified; do not be discouraged,
for the Lord your God will be with you wherever you go.

—Joshua 1:9 (NIV 1984)

I'm in Orlando for a fine arts festival, and I'm just about to go on stage when it happens. Stage fright. Small beads of sweat gather on my forehead, my stomach tightens, and my throat goes dry. Suddenly, doubts about my comedic ability start to wreak havoc with my psyche. And my psyche starts to wreak havoc with me.

Why are you even here? You're not that funny. What makes you think God wants to use you?

My psyche's got a point.

It seems like just a few years ago I was in Alaska and living a satisfied life as a hermit in a cabin that was so remote you had to walk a two-hundred-yard trail through the woods just to reach it. I mean, trick-or-treaters didn't even bother. I had to eat all the candy myself. It was torture.

But I learned a lot during that time. I learned not to feed a moose carrots through an open kitchen window, because their antlers can get stuck. (But it'll give you a great place to hang your dishtowels!) I learned not to bring somebody's lost pet 4-H reindeer in out of the snow just so he can warm up in the cabin while I tracked down the owner. Apparently, reindeer get really nervous when they see a broiler, and they'll destroy your kitchen just trying to escape. And I learned bears don't want you using their skin for a rug. At least, not if they're still using it. Long story.

I loved my life on The Last Frontier and couldn't imagine wanting to live anywhere else. I had no television, no radio, no indoor plumbing; and since it was a homestead, I didn't even have a physical address. No one could find me there.

No one but God. And the IRS. Both seemed to be pretty determined.

It was in that cabin that I accepted Jesus as my Savior and started a personal relationship with Him. I had moved to Alaska to re-examine my life after starting a promising career as an actor and a stand-up comic in Los Angeles. I mingled with Robin Williams, Michael J. Fox, and Whoopi Goldberg, and I enjoyed the accolades that came from my performances and comedy gigs. But the Hollywood lifestyle led me to make some poor choices. I was having fun, but I had no peace.

So, on a whim, I decided to follow a Christian friend to Alaska. My secret plan was to disprove the Bible. I figured if I could do that, then I'd be able to return to my life in L.A. and live the way I wanted without any of the guilt. As all great Christian testimonies invariably say, "God had other plans."

Although I had attended church during my youth, I never had an actual relationship with the Lord. I knew enough to fear Him, though, and I thought we had a mutual understanding that I'd stay out of God's way if He wouldn't turn me into a pillar of salt. I already retained far too much water.

I had always been somewhat of a misfit while growing up, and it seemed like no matter how hard I tried, my attention deficit disorder was always getting me into some kind of trouble. In fact, I can still remember being jealous of those Eskimo kids in Alaska who got to live in igloos. They never got told to go stand in a corner.

It was there in the Alaskan wilderness that God called my name. Not audibly, but it was clear as day to me. I didn't want to face Him at first. I guess you could say I had stage fright with God and for good reason. I can still remember that moment. It felt like God called me by my name—Torry Martin. Not "Boom-Boom," which is the nickname the bullies in high school gave me one day while making fun of me for being overweight. They used to chant that name from the "cool kids" table every time I would walk across the cafeteria. (I've since gotten even with all those bullies. At my last high school reunion, I was the only one who had the same figure now as I had then. Which isn't really saying much, but there's something to be said for consistency.)

After serving the Lord in Alaska for five years, I heard Him call me again. But this time, He was calling me into a comedy ministry. At first I thought He was the one with a sense of humor and that He must be joking, so I avoided His call. That's right. I was draft-dodging the Deity. But only because I couldn't reconcile my pre-Christian past. I couldn't believe God would use someone like me for His glory.

While I was ignoring His call, though, I kept journals. I'd fill the notebooks up with my imagined conversations and adventures. I'd scribble my prayers. I'd write out all the funny things that I would think about or had observed in church on Sunday. And if I wasn't writing, I was reading, but not because I'm the scholarly type. It's just that there wasn't anything else to do in the cabin.

My reading interests ranged from Bible studies, commentaries, and Christian biographies to comic books, how-to-write books, and just about any book on humor that I could get my hands on. When I took the lessons I had learned from my varied reading interests and incorporated that knowledge into my personal journal writing, I started to discover something that ultimately fascinated me. I realized that I could use humor as a tool to teach others about God. More importantly, I also realized through my various Bible studies that God had a history of using people like David and Paul, both of whom had made mistakes in their life and had questionable pasts.

Finally, after avoiding God's call for two years, I wrote my first comedy story, applied a spiritual lesson to it, and then performed it at my church on a Sunday morning. Apparently, it was a success, because they asked me to do it again for the second service. Or, maybe they thought it would just be better if I had more practice. Either way, I felt in my spirit that I had finally answered God's call.

My church supported my endeavors at writing and performing, so a few months later, in an effort to encourage me, they took up a collection to send me to a Christian writing and performing competition in Estes Park, Colorado. I would have been happy with a dinner to encourage me, but they insisted I enter the competition. I'm glad they did because I ended up winning, and that gave me the confidence to trust God and believe that when He calls your name, you really should answer Him. Had my church not faithfully provided the funds for me to attend the competition, my life could have taken a very different path.

Since then, I've had the opportunity to perform my Alaskan-centered "Torry Stories" at churches all across America. I've performed at everything from chili cook-offs to "biker blessings" and from state fairs to cruise ships. I've opened for Pocketful of Rocks, been introduced by Point of Grace, shared the stage with 4Him, and have even opened for Carman. Additionally, I've written seven books of comedy sketches for Lillenas Drama Publishing that are performed in churches all across the United States. I write two monthly humor columns for Christian periodicals. God even opened the door for me to write for Focus on the Family's *Adventures in Odyssey* radio dramas, where I created the character of Wooton Bassett, who also hails from Alaska and is based loosely on my own life and eccentricities. And much to my surprise, I've been featured on several network television shows as well. (No, not on the Food Network. But it is a goal). The point is that it's been an unexpected and exciting journey. Not too bad for someone who has never even tooken a writing class. (Okay, TAKEN a writing class.)

Now I'm a comedian waiting to walk across the stage in front of a crowd of fourteen thousand people. Did you catch that? Fourteen thousand! The same kid who couldn't walk across the school cafeteria without getting made fun of. But they're cheering, not mocking. They're ready to laugh with me, not at me. And I can't wait to laugh with them. I'm just glad that I'm on God's team so I don't have to walk out on that stage alone. I've learned that God truly does make the best comedy partner. He's forgiving, He's loving, and He never steps on a punch line.

I'm still the same me. Insecure in so many ways, still flawed but forgiven, still looking at life just a little off-center, still living life as a self-confessed "hippie for the Holy One," but above all else, I'm still trying my best to overcome my stage fright and answer whenever God calls my name.

TIME TO REFLECT ON GOD'S PROVISION

When all looked lost, it was You, Lord, who saved us!

I am the Lord, the God of all mankind.
Is anything too hard for Me?

—Jeremiah 32:27 (NIV)

25

RESTORATION
Cynthia Howerter

The Lord is near to the brokenhearted
and saves those who are crushed in spirit.
—Psalm 34:18 (NASB)

Being unemployed is like being alone in a desert. The busyness of life is gone, and unscheduled time is left in its place. Time there can either be a curse or a blessing. When Jesus, John the Baptist, and the prophets needed to focus on God, they went into the desert. The innumerable distractions back home that clamored for their attention were gone. In the stillness, they found God. He'd been waiting for them to come unhindered to Him. It's in the desert that we have the opportunity to get to know God. It's where we learn the extent of His love for us. It's where we learn that He knew of our troubles before they happened, and we discover that He's waiting for us to ask for His help.

Even though God provided for all of my family's needs during our nearly two-year period of unemployment, it was

not easy being jobless, having no home of our own, and losing
financial independence. Tim and I learned to lean on the Lord to
lead us through embarrassment, hopelessness, disappointments,
frustration, fearfulness, anxiety, and bouts of despondency and
depression.

Embarrassment: When our money ran low, many people
gave us gift cards for groceries and gasoline, as well as cash. Some
of our doctors provided free visits and medications. The men who
serviced our cars and furnace frequently donated their time and
materials. We would have felt embarrassment in accepting these
gifts and in not being able to pay for services had the man who
annually sold us firewood not explained his reason for helping us:
"What kind of man am I if I won't help you after you've helped
my business for so many years?" His sentiment was echoed by
everyone who provided something for us. God helped Tim, our
kids, and me understand that the help we gave to others through
the years was now being given back to us.

Hopelessness: Prior to this point in my life, I sought other
people's advice whenever I had a problem. God used our season
of unemployment to teach me that He was the One who guided
my life and possessed the wisdom that I needed. Several days after
Tim lost his job, I felt crushed with hopelessness. I desperately
needed God to tell me something encouraging, so I asked Him
to speak to me. He spoke part of a verse from Isaiah: "Those who
wait upon the Lord shall soar like eagles." I clung to this promise,
because I knew that God was telling me how to conquer our
unemployment and financial difficulties. Whenever God spoke
encouragement, I recorded His words in a notebook so I would

remember them and be able to refer to them when I needed inspiration. I learned to speak directly to God whenever I felt hopeless.

Disappointment: Disappointments go hand in hand with financial difficulties and job loss. When our daughter told me that she and her boyfriend were discussing marriage, I realized that Tim and I could not pay for her wedding. The agony I felt at not being able to provide for my daughter's special day drove me to my bedroom floor where I lay sobbing as I poured out my pain to my heavenly Father. Realizing I could not change our financial situation, I handed this wrenching disappointment to the Lord, trusting Him to do what was best for my daughter and us. I also asked the Lord to give me the ability to accept His will with a joyful heart. God heard and answered my prayer: Megan and her boyfriend decided to delay their marriage, and when they finally announced their engagement, my husband was employed.

Frustration: Tim, in particular, often felt frustration when he wasn't getting interviews and another job hadn't appeared. In addition to prayer, Bible, and devotional readings, Tim countered his frustration by choosing activities that he enjoyed. After job searching all morning and eating lunch, Tim went on a fast-paced two-mile walk to retrieve our mail from the post office. In the evening, we frequently walked together, using this time to talk about things that bothered us and to encourage each other. An added benefit of the brisk walks was the production of endorphins that made us feel better. After our evening walk, Tim caught up on reading that he'd had no time for when he was employed. Several times each day, we shared Scriptures and devotional stories with each other as a means to help us see our frustrations from a more positive understanding of them.

Fear and Anxiety: For me, climbing into bed at night opened the door for fearful thoughts and sleep-robbing anxiety. One evening when I asked God to help me stay calm and focused on His provisional power, the word "believe" came to me. I wrote it on a piece of notebook paper and propped it up on our dresser so it was always visible. As soon as the panic from fear and anxiety commenced, I looked at this word and asked myself, "Do you believe God can get you and Tim out of unemployment or not?" My answer was always "Yes." Focusing on what God can do dissolved my fears and removed my anxiety.

Despondency and Depression: God found unique ways to battle the despondency and depression that sometimes threatened Tim and me. He often sent people to refresh our spirits and redirect our focus. Sometimes we'd receive a phone call from a loved one or friend at the exact time we felt forgotten. A number of people invited us to their homes for visits. Their godly wisdom and encouragement, as well as a change in scenery, lifted and renewed our spirits. Family members treated us to restaurant dinners and cookouts, and once when I was particularly discouraged, my sister introduced me to one of her close friends, a Christian woman whose personal stories of God's provision during her difficult times lifted our spirits and infused us with hope.

Marriage: The stresses of unemployment can destroy a marriage. Tim and I understood these potential pitfalls right from the start, and we promised never to blame the other for disappointments or failures. However, even though we tried to manage our stress, we weren't always successful. Once, in great frustration, Tim said, "Cynthia, I hope you soon learn what God wants to teach you so we can get out of this mess."

I was shocked and hurt by my husband's words. Rather than retort with a hurtful emotional response, I quickly asked the Holy Spirit to help me reply. I knew by my gentle question that He answered my request. "Tim, what makes you think there's nothing God wants you to learn?" Tim's jaw dropped and he swallowed hard. "Maybe God needs to teach things to both of us."

Nothing more was said until several weeks later when Tim told me he'd come to realize he had some areas that needed God's attention. We were victims of unemployment, but we were determined that our marriage would not be. With God's help, our trials brought Tim and me closer together and further strengthened our marriage.

Families: Families, too, can disintegrate under the severe stress that unemployment causes. We consistently spoke with our children about the importance of keeping our family strong. During our final meal together in our house on Easter Sunday, our son gave Tim and me a photograph of three combat soldiers. With their arms securely around him, two of the soldiers helped their wounded friend move to safety. Under the picture, Justin wrote, "Our family is a band of brothers going through our own battle right now. Our worth isn't measured by how many times we get knocked down. It's measured by how many times we get back up. We know God is with us and will see us through." I've kept that photograph, and my son's words still move me to tears.

The four of us formed a circle and held hands while we prayed that our family would come through these trials stronger and more tightly knit. And, when our long unemployment period ended and our little band of brothers still stood, closer than ever, we once again formed a circle and praised God for this provision.

Focus on God: After Tim and I moved into Aunt Emma's house, we asked God to tell us what He wanted us to learn through our adversity. We believe one of the reasons our unemployment lasted so long was because God wanted to teach us to seek Him first in all situations. This wasn't something either of us had ever done. We were used to handling problems ourselves, without seeking God's help. It took a lot of time for both of us to unlearn this lifelong behavior and replace it with consistently seeking God in all situations. By the time our period of unemployment ended, seeking the Lord first was ingrained in both of us.

I was at a Christian writers' retreat when Tim called with the news that God gave him a wonderful new job. A shout of elation stuck in my throat as I looked around the crowded lobby. Months before, I had promised God that the second He gave Tim a new job, I would immediately humble myself, lie flat on the floor, and shout praises to Him. The old Cynthia would not have kept this promise, because lying on a floor in a crowded lobby would have humiliated me. However, as I remembered the innumerable ways God faithfully provided for our family in the depths of severe adversity, I overcame all reluctance to keep my promise to God. I got face down on the floor with streams of joyful tears washing my face and shouted praises to my incredible Heavenly Father. Someone knelt next to me and asked if I was all right. I explained that God had just given my husband a job after nearly two years of unemployment. Everyone in the lobby erupted into shouts of thanksgiving and praise to our Heavenly Father.

Our New Life: Several weeks after we moved into our new house, Tim and I talked candidly over cups of coffee. Something still wasn't right, even though God restored Tim's employment and provided a new home in yet another city. We discovered that we both felt numb. We were exhausted. It made sense; we had just gone through twenty-one months of overwhelming turmoil and uncertainty, of our lives completely upended and tossed about. On the one hand, our faith, marriage, and family were stronger than ever, but the difficult journey took a severe toll on us.

We wondered how we would ever recuperate from what we'd gone through. God helped our family recover, but He did it slowly. We still talk about our unemployment experiences with each other, but it's because we want to remember the ways in which God worked on our behalf, as well as the many lessons that He taught us—especially to make Him first and foremost in our lives. There is a confidence that we feel when problems crop up, because we know from our experiences that God will get us through whatever issues we face. Difficulties no longer bring worry or anxiety because we *know* that God can do all He says He can. When Tim's new company recently announced a workforce reduction, we weren't happy to hear it. But our immediate reaction was that if Tim did lose his job, we already knew that God had a wonderful plan for our future and that we could trust Him to work out every detail for us. God's word never returns void to Him, but it accomplishes what He pleases.

Hope for You: If you are unemployed, cling to the knowledge that God knows exactly what you're going through and what you need. He's waiting for you to come to Him—if you haven't already done so. You don't need to have read a single word in the Bible or have stepped inside a church to come to God for His help. All you have to do is talk to Him and ask Him to help you.

Can God get you out of your joblessness or underemployment? Can God improve your financial situation? Can He deliver you from despair? Every writer in this book, including me, has told you from personal experience that He can and He will. All you need to do is ask. God is a God of restoration.

Name has been changed.

Dear Father of All Time,

Thank You for Your provisional grace and power in our lives. Thank You for the promises from Your holy word—reminding us that You will provide for those who put their faith and trust in You. Help us to cling to Your promises and find hope for each day. Teach us to be strong when the tough times of our lives threaten to fill our hearts with fear. Thank You for the many trials You have brought our families through. Although we can't see the future and know without a doubt that we will be financially secure, we know You are enough.

Lord, we pray blessings on each of our readers. We pray that You will keep their hearts encouraged as they experience tough times. Help them recognize Your powerful hand in their own lives as they read each of these stories. Our heart's desire is that each reader will fully seek You. We pray they will find hope and joy for their life journey that is not based on worldly circumstances, but on Your sovereign power to provide all of their needs according to Your great riches in Christ Jesus.

We thank You for leading us to write this book and for each story written. Many are mingled with pain and tears, but each writer has witnessed Your power over the tough times represented throughout the pages of this book.

We pray blessings on each contributing writer and their individual families. Thank You for their willingness to share their powerful stories. We ask You to use them at the highest level You purposed for them from the beginning of time. We know without a doubt You are truly an on-time God who is working to provide … all the time!

May all glory and honor be Yours,

Cynthia and La-Tan

MEET OUR CONTRIBUTING WRITERS

ALYCIA W. MORALES has gone back to working full-time but from home. She serves as Senior Editor of www.InspireAFire.com and works as a freelance editor. She also writes. She's been published by Focus on the Family's *Thriving Family* magazine and ChristianDevotions.us, among others. She also has a devotion in *Faith and Family: A Devotional Pathway for Families*, a publication of Christian Devotions and Lighthouse Publishing of the Carolinas.

When she isn't busy working or packing for a move, she enjoys spending time with her family, reading, taking photos, and drinking decaf coffee. Alycia enjoys encouraging women and can be found doing so in her *Thoughtful Spot* at www.alyciawmorales.com.

BETH K. FORTUNE has a passion for God's Word and a desire to encourage others through writing and speaking. She is a contributing author to Christian Devotions, an online devotion website (http://christiandevotions.us). Beth has published stories in the *Chicken Soup for the Soul* series, as well as the Christian

Devotions book *Faith and Family: A Devotion Pathway for Families.* Some of her articles have been published in Focus on the Family's *Thriving Family* magazine and Dr. Charles Stanley's *In Touch* magazine. Her article "Daddy's Shoes" and poem "Whispers" both won awards at the Blue Ridge Mountains Christian Writers Conference. Beth is a graduate of CLASS (Christian Leaders Authors Speakers Seminar) and Christian Communicators. She is an active member of the Greenville Chapter of Word Weavers and has years of experience serving in women's ministries and teaching Bible studies.

She and her husband live in Mauldin, South Carolina, where they're finding their way as empty nesters. Please visit Beth Fortune's website at www.bethfortune.org.

CARRIE FANCETT PAGELS, Ph.D. writes "romantic" historical fiction and is represented by Joyce Hart of the Hartline Literary Agency. For over two decades, Carrie was a psychologist specializing in child and adolescent issues. Holding a PhD in School Psychology from the University of South Carolina, her doctoral dissertation on step-parenting contains seminal work in understanding relationships between adolescent stepchildren and stepparents. Dr. Pagels coauthored a chapter on Environmental Psychology in a book for Pergamon Press. Her professional reviews have been published in scholarly publications. She is Zone Director of ACFW Mid-Atlantic Region, and continuing as co-chairman of Tidewater-North Area Christian Fiction Writers. Previously, she served as Area Coordinator of ACFW Virginia/West Virginia. She is also a member of Romance Writers of America, the Faith-Hope-Love RWA affiliate group, and FaithWriters. Carrie is the founder and moderator of Colonial American Fiction Writers group. She is also the owner/administrator of Colonial Quills group blog, http://colonialquills.blogspot.com, the owner of Overcoming With God http://cfpagels.blogspot.com, an international group blog, and columnist and contributor of articles to *Voices*—The My Book Therapy E-zine: http://Voices.MyBookTherapy.com. She also writes the "Unsung Heroes" column in The Book Club Network e-zine.

Carrie lives in Virginia with her husband of twenty-five years. Please visit Carrie's website at http://www.carriefancettpagels.com.

CECIL STOKES founded Tentmakers Entertainment in 1999. He has written or produced more than 500 television shows for the following networks: A&E, Court TV, DIY Network, ESPN, Fine Living, Food Network, HGTV, History Channel, TNN, the Travel Channel, and Turner South. For his television programming, Cecil has won Cable Ace, Communicator, New York Film Festival, and Telly awards. He also won an Emmy for his work on the show *Blue Ribbon*. Cecil executive-produced the award-winning documentary *A Man Named Pearl*, as well as *Children of All Ages*. Most recently, Cecil co-created and produced the feature film *OCTOBER BABY*.

DAN WALSH is the award-winning and best-selling author of eight novels published by Revell and Guideposts, including *The Unfinished Gift*, *Remembering Christmas*, and *The Reunion*. For those who haven't read Dan's books, reviewers often compare them to Nicholas Sparks and Richard Paul Evans. His latest project is partnering with Gary Smalley on a four-book fiction series. The first is called *The Dance*. A member of American Christian Fiction Writers (ACFW) and CWG's Word Weavers, Dan now writes full-time, after serving as a pastor for twenty-five years.

He and his wife Cindi have been married thirty-six years and have two grown children, both married, and one grandson. They live in Port Orange, FL. You can follow him on Facebook or Twitter or read his blog. There are buttons to connect to these, as well as previews of all his books, on his website at www.danwalshbooks.com.

DEBORAH RANEY is the author of more than twenty-five novels for the Christian market. Her first novel, *A Vow to Cherish*, inspired the World Wide Pictures film of the same title and launched her career as a novelist after twenty happy years as a stay-at-home mom. Deb's newest novels are from Simon & Schuster.

She and her husband, Ken Raney, have four children and four grandchildren who all live much too far away. Visit Deb on the Web at www.deborahraney.com.

DEE DEE PARKER is a sought-after author and speaker from western North Carolina. She began her writing journey soon after her daughter was diagnosed with breast cancer. Within months, Dee Dee had written her children's book, *Josie Jo's Got to Know*, as a practical way to benefit breast cancer research. Recently featured in the online devotion site *ChristianDevotions*.

us, she is a contributing author for their book, *Faith and Family: A Devotion Pathway for Families*. Dee Dee has contributed to numerous anthologies including *Guidepost's Extraordinary Answers to Prayer: Closer to God, Clothes Lines,* and *Christmas Presence*. A 2011 Christian Communicator's graduate, Dee Dee is a highly-regarded motivational speaker and has appeared before numerous Christian and women's groups. Her work has appeared in Focus on the Family's *Clubhouse Jr.* magazine. She is a member of the leadership team for the Write2Ignite conference for Christian writers of children's literature and often serves as a panel member at book fairs and writing conferences. Dee Dee shares her Appalachian experience on her blog, http://ComeGoHomeWithMe.blogspot.com. Dee Dee has a heart for women and enjoys ministering to the many facets of their lives.

Married to husband Jim, they have a son, Brad, and the cherished memories of their daughter Brooke.

EDDIE JONES is a North Carolina-based writer and Acquisition Editor for Lighthouse Publishing of the Carolinas. He is a three-time winner of the Delaware Writers Conference, and his Young Adult novel, *The Curse of Captain LaFoote*, won the 2012 Moonbeam Award in the Pre-Teen Fiction/Fantasy category and 2011 Selah Award in Young Adult fiction. *Dead Man's Hand*, the first book in the *Caden Chronicles* mystery series, is now available from Zonderkidz.

His latest adult novel, *Bahama Breeze*, is a humorous romantic suspense available from Harbourlight Books. Eddie's recent devotional book, *My Father's Business: 30 Inspirational Stories for Discerning and Doing Gods Will*, features biblical insights and practical applications from the lives of Jeremy Lin, Bruce Wilkerson, George S. Patton, and more.

Eddie is under contract with Zondervan/HarperCollins and is a contributing writer for:

- Common Ground Christian News

- Christian Devotions Ministries

- Inspire A Fire

- CBN.com

He co-writes the He Said, She Said devotions, available at ChristianDevotions.us.

EVA MARIE EVERSON signed her first contract with Barbour Publishing in 1999. Since then, she has attempted to and succeeded at entertaining readers with elements of Southern faith and values. Eva Marie has published more than twenty-five books (both fiction and nonfiction), including:

- *The Potluck Club Series* (with Linda Evans Shepherd) 2005-2007

- *The Potluck Catering Club Series* (with Linda Evans Shepherd) 2008-2011

- *Things Left Unspoken* (Baker/Revell, 2009)

- *This Fine Life* (Baker/Revell, 2010)

- *The Cedar Key Series* (Baker/Revell, 2011-2013)

- *Unconditional* (novelization of the movie by the same
  title) (Broadman & Holman) 2012

Eva Marie is a multiple award-winning author and speaker. She
is one of the original five Orlando Word Weavers critique group
members. She served as the original president from 2000 to 2007
and is now VP of Word Weavers, a national and international
not-for-profit company. During the 2010-2011 school year,
Eva Marie served as an adjunct professor at Taylor University in
Upland, Indiana. She teaches at conferences across the nation. In
2002 and 2009, Eva Marie served as a journalist for Israel Ministry
of Tourism. Her article series, *Falling Into the Bible* (Crosswalk,
2002), served as the inspiration for the multiple-award winning
Reflections of God's Holy Land (Thomas Nelson, 2008), co-written
with Israel's best-selling author, Miriam Feinberg Vamosh.

Born and reared in the low country of Georgia, Eva Marie
is a wife, mother, and grandmother. She lives, works, and finds
respite in her lakefront home in Florida.

FELICIA BOWEN BRIDGES grew up in the Army, living in
eight states and two foreign countries and moving thirteen times
during her first fifteen years of life. A graduate of North Carolina
State University and certified human resources professional,
Felicia is a human resources manager in state government by day
and a Christian fiction writer, editor, and blogger by night. Her
nomadic childhood ignited a passion for travel and missions that
infuses much of her writing. Her novel, *CzechMate*, is the first in a
series of Missionary Kids' Adventures sharing the exciting stories
of young missionaries around the world. She was first published

in 2005 in an anthology of non-fiction short stories titled *Then Along Came an Angel, Messengers of Deliverance.*

Felicia loves being a pastor's wife and mother of four children, ages eleven to twenty-one. Please visit Felicia Bowen Bridges' website: http://Psalms204.blogspot.com.

JAMES L. RUBART is a best-selling, award-winning author of four novels. *Publishers Weekly* says this about his latest release, *SOUL'S GATE*: "Readers with high blood pressure or heart conditions be warned: *this is a seriously heart-thumping and satisfying read* that goes to the edge, jumps off, and 'builds wings on the way down.'" The University of Washington was somehow convinced to give him a degree in Broadcast Journalism back in the mid-80s. He was an on-air talent for a number of years at a Seattle radio station, then sold radio advertising for eight years before starting his own marketing firm in 1994. During the day, he runs Barefoot Marketing, which helps businesses and authors make more coin of the realm.

He lives with his amazing wife and two sons in the Pacific Northwest and loves to dirt bike, hike, golf, take photos, and still thinks he's young enough to water ski like a madman. More at www.jameslrubart.com.

RAMONA RICHARDS, an award-winning writer, editor, and speaker, is the fiction editor for Abingdon Press.

ROGER E. BRUNER worked as a secondary school teacher, job counselor/interviewer, and programmer analyst before retiring from a temporary stint at Target to write full-time. He has two published young adult novels, *Found in Translation* and *Lost in Dreams*, and a quirky mid-life romance—tentatively titled *Impractically Yours*—pending publication in 2013. He has also written seven unpublished novels and a variety of poems, articles, and short plays. Samples of his writing are available at his website, http://www.RogerBruner.com. A guitarist and songwriter, he sings in his church choir, plays bass in the praise team, and plays guitar at a weekly nursing home ministry. He has participated in volunteer mission trips to Romania, England, Wales, and Australia. He uses his blog, http://AsIComeSinging.wordpress.com, to provide free song lyrics to writers who might want to quote them in their own writing.

Roger enjoys spending time with his wife, Kathleen. He has a daughter, who lives with her husband and child in Orlando, and stepdaughters in New York City and Las Vegas. He enjoys reading (especially suspense), web design, photography, and playing Snood.

TAMARA D. FICKAS is a writer by night while working in a hospital business office by day. She has always seen the world in a series of stories and enjoys sharing those stories. In 1997, she had a very personal experience with the living Lord and stepped into the greatest story of all times. It is her desire to use her words to share God's love to a hurting and broken world.

Tamara has written for the reader's section of her local newspaper, several biographies for www.inspirationalchristians. org, and is the coordinator for the American Christian Fiction

Writers of Colorado blog, *The Inkwell*. On her personal blog, www.rockymountainwriter.com, she shares her take on living an abundant life in the Lord. A ten-month period of unemployment helped Tamara see God's provision in action. She hopes this book will bless and help others who are experiencing unemployment.

TORRY MARTIN is an actor, author, screenwriter, humor columnist, comedian, speaker, storyteller, teacher, and an ADHD multi-tasker. He is a member of the Christian Comedy Association and a two-time Christian Artists Gospel Music Association Grand Prize Winner for his acting and writing abilities. Most recently he was awarded the Grand Prize for creating the best "Life Lessons" commercial for The Learning Channel (TLC).

Torry has written for the *Adventures in Odyssey* radio program produced by Focus on the Family and is the creator of Wooton Bassett, a popular character in the series. He additionally writes a regularly featured humor column for Christian periodicals *Clubhouse*, *On Course*, and *Enrichment Journal*. Martin has also had the great pleasure of co-writing several screenplays with his good friend Marshal Younger.

Martin travels nationally speaking and performing stand-up comedy at a variety of Christian events. As an actor, his most recently completed feature films are *The Greater Sins of Lucas Blackstone* and *Adrift*. Torry begins filming his upcoming roles in the faith-based films *Skid* and *My Name is Paul* in early 2013.

MEET THE AUTHORS
CYNTHIA AND LA-TAN

LA-TAN ROLAND MURPHY is a Georgia girl who currently resides in Raleigh, North Carolina with her husband, Joey. La-Tan is an event speaker, freelance writer, and vocalist with a heart for encouraging others. She draws from a wealth of life experiences as a wife, mother, and grandmother—using real life experiences as her greatest sources for speaking and writing inspiration. La-Tan is a regular *Voice* writer for *WHOA Women's Magazine*. The main focus of her heart is celebrating others. This is clearly reflected in her writing and speaking as she lovingly and humorously invites her audience to join her on a journey to discover how to live life to the fullest. If you are interested in booking La-Tan as a keynote speaker or vocalist for an event, please visit her website at: http://www.latanmurphy.com.

CYNTHIA HOWERTER is a Pennsylvania girl who now lives in Virginia with her husband, Tim. She is a member of ACFW (American Christian Fiction Writers) as well as the president of the ACFW Richmond Chapter. Her love for history, especially the American Revolutionary War period, along with being a member of DAR (Daughters of the American Revolution), gives Cynthia a wealth of knowledge to use as a writer. People matter to Cynthia—especially her family, for whom she gave up law school in order to be a stay-at-home mom. Her love for people spills over into her everyday life. She enjoys using her expertise as a genealogist to help others find their roots. Along with speaking at genealogical events, Cynthia has written several genealogical histories about the nearly 8,000 people she has researched. To follow Cynthia's weekly blog posts, please visit her website: *Soar With Eagles* http://cynthiahowerter.com. To book a speaking engagement with Cynthia, you may contact her through her website.

30067809R00152

Made in the USA
Lexington, KY
17 February 2014